Dancing with Ghosts

Dancing with Ghosts

A CRITICAL BIOGRAPHY OF
ARTURO ISLAS

FREDERICK LUIS ALDAMA

UNIVERSITY OF CALIFORNIA PRESS
Berkeley   Los Angeles   London

University of California Press
Berkeley and Los Angeles, California

University of California Press, Ltd.
London, England

© 2005 by the Regents of the University of California

Library of Congress Cataloging-in-Publication Data

Aldama, Frederick Luis, 1969–.
    Dancing with ghosts : a critical biography of Arturo Islas / Frederick
Luis Aldama.
        p. cm.
    Includes bibliographical references and index.
    ISBN 0-520-23188-0 (cloth : alk. paper).—ISBN 0-520-24392-7 (pbk. :
alk. paper)
    1. Islas, Arturo, 1938–   2. Authors, American—20th century—Biogra-
phy.   3. English teachers—United States—Biography.   4. Stanford Uni-
versity—Faculty—Biography.   5. Mexican Americans—Intellectual life.
6. Mexican American authors—Biography.   7. Mexican Americans in
literature.   I. Title.

PS3559.S44Z54   2005
818'.5409—dc22   2004011381

Manufactured in the United States of America
14   13   12   11   10   09   08   07   06   05
10   9   8   7   6   5   4   3   2   1

Contents

Acknowledgments

A month or so into the new millennium I found myself sifting through the Arturo Islas Papers at Stanford's Special Collections Library. An anonymous reader for the journal *Nepantla* had suggested that I might enrich an essay on Islas's posthumously published *La Mollie and the King of Tears* by comparing it to its "original" manuscript. The Islas papers consisted of fifty-two boxes of material—personal correspondence, manuscript drafts, poems, journals, you name it—with the most confidential material sealed till 2009. After I reread the novel's original draft, my curiosity got the better of me. I began requesting box after box of the material, sifting through folder after folder. I do not really believe in destiny, but something about the circumstances was beginning to change my mind. I had to put everything on hold till that summer, but Arturo Islas's story had captured my imagination. Somehow I feel indebted to that anonymous reader—and to serendipity. Of course, the gratitude does not end here. I presented the project proposal to Islas's friend, colleague, and literary executor, Diane Middlebrook. She responded swiftly and with great enthusiasm—even while away doing research in England—by writing letters first to the family for permission and then to library curators Maggie Kimball and Roberto Trujillo to ensure that I would have access to all of the material. Of course, without Roberto Trujillo's foresight back in the mid-1980s, when he first invited Islas to submit material to the archives (see letter February 4, 1985; box 30, folder 3), this project would never have taken form. Thanks to University of California-Santa Cruz Professor Paul Skenazy's last-minute contribution of Islas's journals (1957–91), which were not a part of the Islas Papers and which provided an important addition.

I came to the project mostly as a theorist and not an archivist. Now I really appreciate the importance of archival collections and all the work that those like Maggie, Roberto, Steven, and the others do to smooth the way for research projects. Many thanks to Marcy McAugh, whose offer to transcribe interviews with Islas's family and friends gave me a necessary reprieve from carpal tunnel pain.

Of course, the task of archiving, typing, interviewing, and organizing is but one of many. I am especially grateful to UC-Berkeley Comparative Literature Department's Victoria Yost for her generous support through the many years. Colleagues and friends Mimi Gladstein, Cecilia Burciaga, Herbie Lindenberger, and Ruth Watt helped fill in blanks and affirmed the multifaceted quality of Islas's personality. Like a many-surfaced crystal, he refracted different shades of the spectrum to different audiences.

UC Press editor Linda Norton's early enthusiasm and backing helped convince John Stevenson, chair of English at the University of Colorado-Boulder, of the project's importance; I thank him and the University of Colorado for giving me the time off to write the book. Randy Heyman at UC Press helped pave the way for the project's publication. And I appreciate the critical feedback from UC-Berkeley Professors José David Saldívar and Francisco Lomelí. My brother, Professor Arturo J. Aldama, continues to be one of my great pillars of support. Thanks also to Dagmar Logie of Stanford's English department, who furnished a year-long extension long after Stanford library postdoctoral borrowing privileges had expired, allowing me to finish the job.

Many of my friends and family put their needs aside to help me during this intense period of writing. Warm *abrazos* to Islas's parents, Jovita and Arturo Islas, as well as to his brother Mario, for their generous hospitality and willingness to tell me stories. Deep gratitude goes to my father, Luis, for his support and sharp eye, and to Christopher Scott Powell, for dropping everything to help the process run a smooth course.

Finally, I dedicate this book to the late Barbara Christian (December 12, 1943–June 15, 2000). Like Arturo Islas, she was a professor, an intellectual, a creative spirit, and a role model who touched and inspired those around her.

Introduction

From an early age, Arturo Islas had an eerie understanding of his own mortality. He experienced several life-threatening illnesses and, as a child raised Catholic in a Chicano family in El Paso, was constantly reminded of the precariousness of bodily existence. To survive not only a religious culture of death but also his personal sense of mortality, Islas learned to use language creatively, to ironize and thereby transcend death. As he designed psychological spaces within which to manipulate temporal categories, he reshaped linear time into a more dynamic helical framework. These fictional realms vitalized and enriched his fifty-two years in the world. For Islas, ghosts (especially those passed down through family legends) lived in the present as part of life's continuum.

The title of this book—*Dancing with Ghosts*—alludes not only to Islas's approach to life/death but also to this biography's approach to its subject. Like Islas's novels, poems, and short stories, which hybridize both time (past, present, and future) and space (north and south of the border), the chapters of the biography are thematic clusters that speak across time and space, unrestricted by linear causality. They unfold in a kaleidoscopic manner that captures the way Islas wrote about and experienced the world. The story I tell dances, so to speak, between childhood and adulthood, past and present, thereby sidestepping conventional biographical teleologies and highlighting the fact that Islas lived as if time were nonlinear. In the dynamic of this biography, as in Islas's life, memories behave irrespective of chronology and a single life holds a multiplicity of living selves.

More practically speaking, Islas's sense of mortality also led him to use language to preserve everything he thought and felt. He sought to slow down time by creating vortexes of textualized experience. He kept journals to chart the deep psychological conflicts he felt as a closeted gay college student at Stanford in the late 1950s; he documented virtually every thought and event, on one occasion transcribing his coming-out phone conversation with his parents. He absorbed and reflected on paper the pain and ecstasy of inhabiting in-between spaces: Spanish/English, white/brown, gay/straight, institution/family, San Francisco/El Paso, and academic/Chicano activist, to name a few. From these many worlds Islas drew a complex and irreducible network of selves.

NOVELIST, POET, PROFESSOR

This book could have been a hagiography, given Arturo Islas's achievements. He studied his way out of El Paso, Texas, to become the first Chicano to graduate (Phi Beta Kappa, no less) from Stanford in 1960. It was not until long after the post–civil rights 1960s that Stanford's affirmative action policy turned its sights toward Mexican Americans and African Americans. Affirmative action in Islas's day included a laissez-faire move to diversify along lines of gender, religion, or race. Islas's BA with honors in English (and minor in religious studies) proved his mettle. He went straight into the PhD program in English and, after taking some time off in the late 1960s (he worked as a speech therapist at a Veterans

Administration hospital), became one of the first Chicanos to earn a doctorate in English. Soon after a brush with death that left Islas without a colon and with what he called a "shit bag" at his side for the rest of his life, Stanford's English department hired him on as a professor. Launching into a career as a teacher, scholar, and creative writer, he wore the garb of a Stanford faculty member and remained the only Chicano professor in English until his death. He worked actively to clear a space for new Mexican American undergraduates, developing proto-Chicano-studies courses and Chicano-friendly administrative policies. Along with the few other Chicanos in academia—Renato Rosaldo, Al Camarillo, and Tomás Ybarro-Frausto—he would help build the Chicano Research Center to fund and support young Chicano/a scholars.

Islas, however, did not exactly follow a 1970s brown-power ideological line. He made efforts to keep politics separate from cultural-aesthetic endeavors, though he understood why traditionally marginalized groups identified the personal as political. He saw in many of the poems, novels, and short stories Chicanos wrote (at the time few works by Chicanas were published) an overreliance on a mystical *raza*-Aztlán spirituality or folklore without a lasting, aesthetic quality to redeem them. We must remember that Islas trained as a critic and poet largely under the aegis of the aesthete Yvor Winters. He was one of the first to articulate an aesthetic that would bridge Anglo, Latin American, Chicano, and European storytelling styles and voices; he theorized a writerly tradition of forms and bodies both white and brown, Spanish and *indio*, to rupture divisions between cultural paradigms. Islas's first literary endeavors—his short stories, poetry, and the 1976 draft of a novel, "Día de los muertos" (Day of the dead; box 5, folders 4–7)—also blurred boundaries between straight and queer sexual identification. In "Día de los muertos" Islas invented one of the first narrator-protagonists who were overtly gay and Chicano (the most notable earlier one is in John Rechy's 1963 *City of Night*). As this work splintered into "American Dreams and Fantasies" (intended as a series of vignettes; box 12, folders 1–8) and what would become his first published novel, *The Rain God: A Desert Tale* (1984), it gave subtle texture to a queer Chicano narrative voice. It broke with the formulaic migrant-farmworker or out-of-the-ghetto mold. To this day, Chicano/a authors celebrate Islas's effort to challenge the mainstream publishers' stranglehold on "ethnic" fiction. For the author Denise Chávez, Islas's overcoming the obstacle of publishing *The Rain God* helped pave the way for writers "with passion and energy" to emerge and for the general public to encounter the "power of Latino literature" (interview with Chávez, March 2001).

COMPLICATED TEXTURES

This laundry list of "firsts" tells only part of Islas's story—the part that reads like an exemplary resumé or a possible hagiography. But Arturo Islas was much more complex than a series of academic honors and glossy surfaces. The biographer's task is to see beyond Islas's sensational and melodramatic "up-from-the-bootstraps" story and its tragic denouement; his conflictive impulses, desires, and feelings are at once uncommon and common. He responded instinctively and not always rationally to a world marked by grand paradox, irony, and injustice. He was gentle, soft-spoken, and generous; and he carried a deep love for his friends, lovers, and family. He was also narcissistic, self-pitying, temperamental, moody, unpredictable, and manipulative. Many clichés might apply to Islas's life: polio as a child, a scrape with death in his early thirties, and the fatal struggle with AIDS in the late 1980s. Hence my task is to acknowledge the complex layers—both ordinary and extraordinary—of his life.

Irreducible to a unified self, Islas existed within different public and personal spaces. In the San Francisco 1970s S&M and bathhouse scene he was queer and preferred being "dominated." As a professor of English literature at Stanford, he was quite at home in the liminal area between white-establishment expectation and racialized politicking. The different chapters in this book explore some of Islas's fundamental selves—Islas as a son and brother, Islas as a body subject to a variety of epidemics, Islas as a same-sex-desiring being, Islas as a Chicano—to trace how his sense of the private shifted within larger historical and social movements. How does Islas define himself as a Chicano in the 1970s and the 1980s, or in a Stanford classroom and again at his family's dinner table in El Paso? Sex-

uality, racial identification, and political personality all intersect to dif-
ferent degrees in differently constructed public spaces at different junc-
tures. This biography seeks out these highlighted modes of being within
which Islas's life unfolds.

Concerning his racial private/public persona, Islas embraced the 1970s
Chicano rhetoric of brown power, knowing that a certain amount of es-
sentializing had to be done to make Chicanos/as visible. Yet he was also
cautious of the Chicano movement's us/them, white/brown binary and
queer-unfriendly rhetoric (his own sense of self as a gay man found sanc-
tion and support among a white San Francisco crowd). As a professor at
Stanford, he was well aware of his cultural and academic power to help
shape a new reality for Chicanos/as. He helped push affirmative action
through at Stanford and persuaded the university to replace a white,
male-author-dominated "Western Culture" course with "Cultures, Ideas,
and Values," which included writers and thinkers of color. He was the first
to create Chicano literature courses—ex nihilo. He helped mold a second
generation of Chicano/a creative writers (the novelist Ben Sáenz as well
as the poets Francisco Alarcón and Bernice Zamora) and professors (José
David Saldívar, currently at UC-Berkeley, and Rafael Pérez-Torres, cur-
rently at UC-Los Angeles, for example) to cultivate a legacy of Chicano
letters that would live and grow. Yet he did not want to endorse hierar-
chies of racial difference. For Islas, it was always better to build bridges
than barricades. Thus he began to articulate a worldview where forms
(racial, aesthetic, and political) jostle and mingle to reflect complexity.

Islas turned to literature (and not science, as he had originally in-
tended) to dislodge the heteronormative, racially essentialist categories
(white/Spanish as pure vs. brown/Chicano/*indio* as impure) that de-
limit our experience in the world. Islas's bridge building carried over into
a crafting of his own aesthetic. From his early short stories, written while
he was an undergraduate, to his mature novels, written toward the end
of his life, Islas invented worlds where fact blended with fiction, south-
western border towns alternated with San Francisco city spaces. Islas
worked to create an aesthetic that both reflected his life and represented
the complex array of epistemological and ontological influences on him
and others around him. His novels, poems, and short fiction hybridized

form (southwestern gothic, pre-Columbian myth, and Latin American magical realism), language (Spanish and English), and sexuality (gay, straight, and bisexual). They depicted that unstable place of "the bridge [where] home is a temporary pause on the way somewhere else" that would unsettle readers' categories of being and knowing (fifth annual Ernesto Galarza lecture; box 30, folder 1).

Islas had written much fiction and poetry by 1976, when he finished "Día de los muertos," but planned that "Día" would be his first publicly visible work to reflect the "pause" between different racial, sexual, and social spaces—a textual borderland. (His other writings had only circulated among his colleagues, friends, and workshop attendees.) But Islas's gay/straight, El Paso/San Francisco scenes made mainstream editors so uncomfortable that they refused to publish the novel. A mid-1970s New York publishing climate had not caught up with the change in the ethnosexual climate. By the time Islas did publish a version of "Día," he had received letters of harsh rejection for over a decade. Those that overlooked the same-sex sexuality pointed to an overreliance on Spanish; in fact only a handful of Spanish words appear in this manuscript. Islas transformed "Día de los muertos" into the more "sanitized" *The Rain God* (published in 1984 by a small house, it achieved a word-of-mouth success), but his borderland fictions continued to disconcert. Publishers also refused his second novel, *La Mollie and the King of Tears.* (It was rejected, ironically, by the very house that would publish it posthumously.) Islas made his breakthrough with *Migrant Souls,* a follow-up to *The Rain God* that William Morrow finally published in 1990.

For Islas, writing was not just about articulating an aesthetic that spoke to an in-between way of being and knowing. It was a form of healing. Writing became Islas's way of understanding and gaining control over his past and present traumas—especially his destructive relationship with his great love, Jay Spears. Writing also offered the possibility of returning to his place of origin: the southwestern desert. In his writing, Islas returned to the desert again and again because of its emancipating anonymity and because it lacks markers separating language and body. Islas used his writing to find the barren place that nourished his soul.

(Even in the city-based *La Mollie,* the narrator-protagonist is from El Paso.) The desert was an enduring presence for Islas—both in his writing and in his psyche. Through multifarious avenues of expression, he would constantly refresh his thirst for the desert.

METHODOLOGY

Islas's life story, sketched above, could fuel a sensationalist biography that would mar rather than enrich an understanding of Islas's many identities and experiences. I seek instead to detail the contours of Islas's life in ways that go beyond clichés (macho father traumatizes son, who experiences sexual "confusion" during puberty and dysfunctional relationships and drug addiction as an adult). Each chapter considers Islas's identity as a self with an artillery of responses to specific stimuli. This biography, therefore, responds to the different moments and selves that make up Islas. It employs a variety of critical prisms—humanistic, psychoanalytic, and sociohistoricist, for example—according to the contextual demands.

Islas was a scholar who believed that theories and frames for reading grow out of close textual analysis. In this spirit, I respond to the facts and fictions of his life and narrate them as accurately as possible. Sometimes a psychoanalytic reading percolates to the surface and at other times a borderland theory of racial identity emerges. The narrative of his life and the critical framing of his work inform each other.

Islas's story reflects the changing tides of the sexual politics and culture of late twentieth-century gay liberation and oppression in the United States. It also moves between the realms of individual memory (personal journal entries) and a larger American mainstream's multicultural revision of white, male memoirs. For example, Islas responded with vitriol (privately and publicly) to Richard Rodriguez's *Hunger of Memory,* published in 1982, because as far as Islas was concerned, Rodriguez's anti-bilingual education and anti-affirmative action politics reductively essentialized an otherwise complex Chicano/a experience of ethnicity and class in the United States. Here Islas's visceral reaction distances him from the first ethnic attempts to justify a system that still disenfranchises those who have traditionally been at the political and cultural margins.

This is not to say that Islas was against the mainstream. He was a gay Chicano who identified strongly with the canonical bodies of knowledge and culture and the most widespread values in America. He enjoyed watching the Superbowl as much as he enjoyed watching a documentary such as *The Times of Harvey Milk*; for him, reading Fitzgerald's *Great Gatsby* was as pleasurable and inspiring as reading Ron Arias's *Road to Tamazunchale*. And Islas had his fair share of 1980s Yuppie abandon: he snorted many a line of cocaine, he took part in "purification" rituals and spent money (often in the form of a gift from his friend Ethel Hoffman) on "authentic" New Age health-spa retreats in New Mexico's Santa Fe and in California's Santa Cruz mountains.

As I already noted, Islas conceived of writing as a blurring of private with public, fiction with fact. This was the case even in his journal's most private entries, where he invented an older-brother character, Beto, who was the object of the father's affections. Also, he designed the many selves fiction presents for specific audiences. Conversely, the facts of everyday life—historical events like the murder of his closeted uncle Carlos by a "straight" white soldier the night of February 19, 1967—would find their way through fault lines of emotion onto the pages of his novels, short stories, and poetry. His life was a performance that constantly melted fiction into fact and fact into fiction; in a sense, he wrote fiction and fiction wrote him. He defined his novels, for example, as autobiographical fiction. With this in mind, I move fluidly between the facts of his life and the fictions he created, mindful of the ways in which each realm created and was created by the other.

Some of the material I use might reveal sensitive truths about family and friends: details about family affairs, Islas's experimental sexual activity, and so on. I'm careful to reveal the private only when it enriches an understanding of Islas. As Diane Middlebrook candidly wrote of her use of Anne Sexton's therapy session transcripts, "The dead cannot have wishes, they can only have wills, and wills delegate the responsibility for making decisions" (1996, 127). When Islas donated his records to Stan-

ford, they became the property of the larger Chicano and American pub-
lic record. While the most private documents—journals, epistolary ex-
changes, and letters of recommendation—were to remain sealed till the
year 2009, he nonetheless gave them with the idea that they would help
document his life so the public could understand it better. Access to the
contents before the 2009 date certainly allowed for the earlier publication
of this biography. But it did not change certain ethical rules of engaging
and making public such private material. For example, I left out details
such as people's names—and in some cases, even private correspon-
dence—that might defame or hurt individuals who are still living. While
some of this information might add to our understanding of one aspect
or other of Islas's life, its potential to harm these individuals proved too
great.

Biography is both a subjective and objective performance. Its task is
to balance empathetic engagement with the distance necessary to
look critically at an individual's life. In this dual process—critical and
absorptive—I believe I succeeded, moving back and forth between the
"subjective," which anchors the story in the local and personal, and the
"objective," which might appeal to an audience beyond myself or Islas.

This biography makes visible the participation of those at the mar-
gins—gay and Chicano/a—in the continued formation of American his-
tory and culture. Islas's story has the traditional Horatio Alger story ele-
ments but follows a sexually and racially outlawed subject's struggles to
succeed on an everyday local level and far beyond. Islas's shape-shifting
story expands our cultural memory and denaturalizes hierarchies of eth-
nic and sexual difference. Islas's life invites the reader to reexamine the
social prejudices that still prevail in the United States.

"Nothing is ever ours," Islas writes in a journal entry (June 20, 1974).[1]
To tell Islas's story is not to shine a single light that completely exposes
him but rather to illuminate a web of vibrant hues and shades that mix to
suggest impressionistically an array of complex details. *Dancing with
Ghosts* retraces the trajectory of a writer, scholar, and teacher who be-
lieved in the act of recovery (narrating, remembering, and forgetting) as
he hybridized genres and invented subjectivities to express a manifold
queer Chicano/a poetic self.

Arturo Islas was born to Arturo Islas Sr. and Jovita La Farga on May 25, 1938, in El Paso, Texas. He was the first of three sons. He grew up in El Paso and spent his undergraduate and graduate student years, as well as his career as professor and writer, in the San Francisco Bay Area. He died on February 15, 1991, at his home in Palo Alto.

The several very different worlds of Islas's experience helped shape his complex personality. His early experiences as a child and adolescent in El Paso and his years as a student at Stanford University all contributed to a constantly shifting sense of self. As he recollects in a journal entry on April 20, 1987: "I have so many selves and wear so many hats. The 'Self' in self esteem has nothing to do with ego, with me, with all those roles I play throughout a day. It is the self of quiet attention to what is around me and within me, a calm that has an inner eye over which I have no control."

Islas's initial experience growing up on the border of Texas and Mexico raised issues of class, race, sexuality, gender, and religion. His paternal grandmother, Crecenciana Sandoval, was in her teens when she met, fell in love with, and married the much older Jesús Islas. Both lived in Chihuahua, Mexico, but hailed from places north and south of the border: Crecenciana was from San Miguel de Allende, Mexico, and Jesús was from Las Cruces, New Mexico. In Chihuahua, Crecenciana was working as a schoolteacher and Jesús in commerce when Mexico's historical tides shifted—for the worse. In 1910 the Mexican Revolution, no longer an echo in the distance, closed in on their community. Islas would recollect (in one of his many collage-memories passed down through the family's strong oral tradition) how Crecenciana and Jesús's firstborn, Arturo Islas—"a true intellectual, man, hero, and perhaps (if all tales are true) our only poet"—was shot dead by a Federalist bullet (journal, August 2, 1959). Their son's tragic death in his twenties spurred Crecenciana and Jesús to seek refuge in Juárez, the northern city that shared the border with El Paso. As the revolution lurched toward its end, Jesús worked his way up the political ladder and became the city treasurer, while Crecenciana continued to teach. According to family lore, as the war approached the northern territories, Pancho Villa pulled Jesús Islas aside and told him to move across the border to El Paso, or they might witness another tragic loss. They crossed the Rio Grande, from "one bloody side of the river to the other and into a land that just a few decades earlier had been Mexico" (1990b, 42). Across the border, they became the migrant souls Islas would later write about. In El Paso, four years after a second Arturo Islas was born (the parents named him to honor the memory of the first son), Jesús died. Crecenciana was left the task of raising the ten surviving children on her own—though she had help from her two sisters, who had also settled along the El Paso/Juárez border.

The family survived the Mexican Revolution and settled into the social and cultural borderland that was El Paso. Crecenciana Sandoval was a feisty survivor who ruled her household with an iron fist. She worked for a dry-goods store and as a teacher. After retiring, she would dip into her pension to put food on the table. Her hard discipline taught her children the importance of education: reading, writing, arithmetic, and fluency in Spanish and English. In the end, the matriarch's struggle paid off. The new generation of bilingual, bicultural Islas children moved swiftly through the social ranks because of their education. In *Migrant Souls* Islas's narrator calls these figures (fictionalized) "border Mexicans with American citizenship" (1990b, 42). And though they bumped up against an Anglo-owned glass ceiling, the second generation's education and bilingual fluency opened doors into careers in an El Paso world otherwise dominated by Anglos. Arturo Islas Sr. became well respected as one of four Mexican Americans in an Anglo police force, for example. Crecenciana's belief in education passed down the line to the third generation. As each generation grew, its members also moved into traditionally Anglo-dominated occupations: Islas and his cousins went to college, with four earning postgraduate degrees that opened careers in law and academia.

The dust-swept El Paso border town was far from a Mexican migrant utopia. The prejudice against Mexicans (not always Anglo-generated) was like the constant heat waves that rippled in the El Paso air. Within it the strong matriarch Crecenciana and her "very intelligent" sisters reproduced their own hierarchies of difference. Crecenciana and her sisters had internalized an assortment of ethnic prejudices based on a pure (Spanish)/impure (*indio*) duality. Applying this dichotomy circulated by the *criollo* Mexican elite—internalizing myths of whiteness and purity identified as Euro-Spanish—Crecenciana carefully stayed out of the sun to keep her skin *güera,* that is, a light olive complexion allowing her to lay claim to a pure Spanish blood line (though in fact, she was a shade of chocolate brown). She told young Islas that the Spanish she was making sure he spoke without a hint of an accent was pure Castilian and not the impure Mexican dialect. Islas was taught that only the Spanish side of his heritage was to be preserved. In *The Rain God*, Islas's narrator reflects how "the indian in them was pagan, servile, instinctive rather than intellectual, and was to be suppressed, its existence denied" (1984, 142). In Crecenciana's internalized racial paradigm, darkness was equated with dirt, impurity, sin.

Of course, this internalizing of a Euro-Spanish/*indio* duality caused rifts between Crecenciana and other family members. For example, she loved Islas deeply. He was *güero,* male, and the first grandchild to be fluent in her pure "Castilian" tongue. (Had she lived long enough to discover that Islas was gay, she would have cast him aside as a *desgraciado* and an *indio*—no matter what his skin tone or how "accentless" his Spanish.) And when Crecenciana's sister Jesusita gave birth "out of wedlock" to her son Alberto, she became a family outcast—an impurity (interview with Jovita Islas). In protest, Jesusita crossed back over the Rio Grande with her man and that, as far as her sister was concerned, was akin to becoming a tramp. The other sister, Virginia, discarded this pure/impure myth, living her life unwed with her partner in a house filled with hundreds of cats. Sadly, Crecenciana had internalized a worldview she could not enact. She could not afford to hire an *india,* for example, to wash dishes and clean house. Often, because she refused to dirty her hands, she would let the filth pile up around her. Working hard at the Spanish *señora* look, she'd wear black clothes and gloves that stifled her in the hot desert sun.

Islas spent a great deal of his early childhood with Crecenciana, absorbing an appreciation both for education and for his mythologized European descent. His mother, Jovita, hailed from a family less governed by rigid hierarchies. Though Islas did not know his mother's father, Conrado La Farga, or her mother, Virginia García, their influence was evident in the family, and Islas would seek refuge in Jovita for protection against his father's iron-fisted rule. To survive, Jovita had learned to see beyond the duality to appreciate the many shades that exist in the entire spectrum. Throughout a life filled with crises, Jovita found strength by bending with rather than resisting the world.

Conrado La Farga was born and raised in the small Mexican fishing village of Culiacán. With his sights on the bigger and better, he went to El Paso to ply his trade as a cigar maker. After the cigar-making factory closed, he and his young wife, Virginia García, along with their daughter, Antonia, went to California. They would soon discover that in an early twentieth-century San Francisco the job opportunities were just as scarce as in El Paso. The city's cold climate and unfriendly culture did not suit Conrado's Mexican-oriented tastes. Soon after the death in infancy of their son Ramón, first Virginia and then Conrado went back to the

warmer and more brown-hospitable El Paso. But the San Francisco so-
journ had already chilled them to the bone; they returned to El Paso with
the tuberculosis that would later take both their lives. Virginia died at
twenty-nine, when Jovita and Esperanza were still quite small. Conrado
died at the age of fifty-seven, having raised Jovita and her younger sister,
Esperanza, with the help of his oldest child, Antonia.

Like many Mexicans living in El Paso during the first half of the twen-
tieth century, Jovita La Farga grew up in the district of El Paso known as
El Segundo Barrio, which edged the U.S./Mexican border and was far
from the city's Anglo elite. After Conrado died, Antonia took over the
parenting of Jovita and Esperanza; their aunts Carolina and Francisca
also lived in El Paso but were tangled up in their own lives and rarely
saw the girls. Unfortunately, the mother and father's fate also became
Antonia's. Soon after she married a World War I veteran who had been
diagnosed with an arrested case of tuberculosis; she contracted the dis-
ease and died when she was twenty-six years old. In the absence of an
older parental figure, the teenagers Jovita and Esperanza sought comfort
in each other. Together, they mourned the deaths of their parents and
their older sister.

Death and suffering wrapped themselves thickly around Jovita's early
life, but she refused to turn away from the world. Attending El Paso High
in the mid-1930s, Jovita met and fell in love with Arturo Islas (Sr.).
Though she had been dating another boy from the barrio, she was taken
with Arturo Islas's striking good looks, dazzling charisma, and bad-boy
attitude: "Arturo was bad. He would go to the dances and crash the
dance with his gang of friends" (interview with Jovita Islas). He was the
high school football jock whose swagger and sure-footedness (he was
Crecenciana's son, after all) won over Jovita; her life had been full of in-
stability and loss, and Arturo radiated confidence. In turn, Jovita's
beauty and look of innocence won him over. After first seeing her in a his-
tory class, he pursued her tirelessly. Her inaccessibility was a challenge;
she had a boyfriend and was seemingly distant (as his mother was). Islas
(Jr.) fictionalized this courtship: his mother "was not easy prey, and she
did not use the usual devices the other girls employed when they played
at refusing his large and insatiable cock" ("Día de los muertos"; box 5,

folder 4). Arturo was certain that Jovita would become his wife and the mother of his children. And she did. They graduated from El Paso High, married, and began their new life together. Jovita used her typing skills and went to work for $30 a week at the local American Optical Company. Arturo trained to become a policeman. With a child on the way and with money saved, they bought a house of their own five blocks north of the barrio, on Almagordo Street, where their neighbors were Mexican Americans, African Americans, and some older Anglos. Here there were no signs, "No Mexicans Allowed," like those in shop windows a few blocks closer to the downtown.

When Jovita discovered that she was pregnant, she went back and forth between being angry and ecstatic. In a collage-memory, Islas writes,

> [My mother] was not ready to have children and had wanted to dance and party with my father for at least the first two years of their life together. Both were born and brought up Mexican Catholics and were joined together for all eternity at Immaculate Conception Church in El Paso, Texas. I entered into this "valle of tears" (a phrase from one of my favorite prayers to the Virgin Mary . . . "Hail Holy Queen") exactly nine months and two days later. Of course, when I was born and she saw me, my mother either forgot or repressed her anger and there is a baby picture of me in the chest of family photos with one of those sickly sweet Hallmark card poems in the corner that describes me as a blossom that fell from heaven. (Flannery O'Connor lecture; box 25, folder 11)

Nicknamed "Sonny" (a popular name for Mexican Americans in El Paso at the time), Arturo would later become his mother's confidant and supporter in a household ruled by a patriarch.

LIFE IN THE BARRIO

With their firstborn, Jovita and Arturo settled into the affordable working-class neighborhood of the Five Points Area. Arturo made the most of his salary as a policeman by using his passport to cross the El Paso/Juárez border; in Juárez he could buy cheaper food and household supplies. Even so, the young family would not have enough money to provide the building blocks for their child's future. To give their son all the opportunities open to him, they would need money for schooling. Jovita set aside money from her part-time secretarial job, later using these funds to help pay for clothes, books, and other school supplies; some of this money also went to pay the Mexicanas from *el otro lado* for cleaning, cooking, and helping raise Sonny. In *The Rain God*, Islas's thinly veiled autobiographical voice recalls one such helper:

> María was one of hundreds of Mexican women from across the border who worked illegally as servants and nursemaids for families on the American side. Of all ages, as young as thirteen or fourteen, they supported their own families and helped to rear the children of strangers with the care and devotion they would have given their own relatives had they been able to live with them. One saw these women standing at the bus stops on Monday mornings and late Saturday night. Sunday was their only day off and most of them returned to spend it on the other side of the river. (1984, 13)

With the help of the many Marías who came and went, the father and especially the mother could work longer hours; the family could then afford to give Sonny the opportunities he would need in order to realize the American dream.

While Jovita was at work and Sonny under the watchful eye of a maid, Arturo was honing his skill as a policeman—patrolling, sleuthing, and incarcerating. As the *El Paso Herald* news reporter and family friend Earl Shorris recalls, Arturo Islas achieved "near legendary stature as a policeman" and became known "as the smartest detective, the toughest cop, the best diplomat with other law enforcement agencies" (1992, 99). Arturo Sr.'s public and private worlds grew increasingly alike. He kept his own household under tight surveillance too. Islas recalls, "I thought about the times he settled any arguments by simply unbuckling his revolver and placing it on the table during lunch, or at least, that's what I thought he was doing" ("The Loneliest Man in the World"; box 9, folder 17). True to the Crecenciana iron-fist tradition, he was a strong, macho man who ruled with a stubborn and strict hand.[1] Jovita said he "was a little bit on the hard side. Discipline, you know?" (interview). Perhaps Arturo's acceptance of Crecenciana's worldview helped him. His two brothers, Carlos and Enrique, struggled against Crecenciana's black/white, saint/sinner world-view and ended up unhappily. Carlos was forced to closet his gay sexuality and was murdered by a "straight" soldier. Like many other young men in El Paso in the 1940s, Enrique chose to identify as a zoot-suiter ("I remember admiring his duck tail haircut," wrote Islas for a lecture on Chicano literature) and died a bitter, drunken man in east Los Angeles (box 32, folder 15).

Arturo Islas was especially emotionally distant from Sonny—the first-born who would fail to live up to fatherly expectations. The father worked long hours as a policeman patrolling the streets and in his spare time fixed cars and played handball at the El Paso YMCA: he was all physicality. The son increasingly shunned such activity: he sought stasis and quietude, discovering adventure and mystery in novels and history books. (As I relate in chapter 3, when Islas and his brother Mario left home, both chose professions the father's macho code regarded as "effeminate": the first becoming a writer/professor and the second a priest. And finally, far from their father's surveillance, both came out of the closet.)

While Spanish was the primary language used at home, young Islas learned to read, write, and speak English from an early age. This was both a result of Crecenciana's tutoring and a consequence of attending the neighborhood elementary schools. First at Alta Vista and then at Houston Grade School, Sonny and all his Mexican American classmates had Anglo teachers who taught in English. Texas was the first state in the country to organize a struggle in the 1940s for equality for Mexican Americans in public schools, but even when state legislative policies were enacted, they were rarely enforced within local districts. Anglo schoolchildren—in spite of struggles to desegregate districts by civil rights groups and pressure by the Mexican government to promote a bilingual curriculum—still went to schools in other neighborhoods. But Sonny, with the help of his grandmother, who acted as disciplinarian and English tutor, advanced swiftly through his English-only elementary school—though he always feared failure and felt estranged from his fellow students, most of whom spoke only Spanish.[2] He learned to speak, read, and write in English well in advance of his age.

The parents did not want their son to know only English and to acquire only American customs and thus lose sight of a fundamental aspect of his identity: his Mexican heritage and its accompanying customs, history, and values. So, though his parents spoke English well, they insisted on speaking Spanish at home. During meals they often told him stories about his ancestors to instill in him a sense of pride in his culture.

Sonny was studious in and o⟨ ⟩ of the classroom from an early age. After school, Sonny would spend time with his reading, writing, and arithmetic, sitting in the kitchen as his mother confided in him the family's secrets and her problems with the largely absent and emotionally distant husband and father. Jovita lavished attention on him (particularly after he contracted polio at age eight), and Sonny returned his mother's love, feeling that she was the only one he could discuss personal problems with. He could, for example, talk to his mother about teasing at school. As a young boy, Islas was very sensitive about his ears; he would often be teased about how they stuck out, and at one point even considered using his father's razor to cut them off. Yet while Sonny bonded deeply with his mother, he also felt increasingly uneasy about her frequent gestures, sighs, and comments about her self-sacrifice, discomfort, and sense of victimization as the wife of Arturo Sr. As the boy came of age he learned to keep her emotional baggage at arm's length.

Home involved a complex tangle of emotion for Sonny, so he often found alternate places for solace. He regularly punched his library card and turned readily to the Catholic Church: "there was not a day that the Church and its teachings were not a part of my conscious and unconscious life" (Flannery O'Connor lecture; box 25, folder 11). From an early age, Islas demonstrated a deep piety and devotion, making head altar boy at St. Patrick's Cathedral in El Paso. His regular church and library attendance was not just a means to get away from a difficult home, but also a way to control a growing temper—he would often flare up at his younger brother Mario ("Pee Wee") for not eating or praying correctly or not showing enough piety in church. Immersing himself in the life of the church and school, he hoped, would keep him from resembling his father as he grew up.

Turning to the Catholic Church was both a way to gain his parents' approval and a place to practice self-control and self-restraint. It was also a space of the imagination. As a child he witnessed the seasonal pilgrimages in which hundreds of devout Catholics wore placards of the Virgin

Mary and other saints, mumbled prayers, stroked rosaries, and mysteriously disappeared as they made their way up the Cristo Rey mountain to pay respect to a fifty-foot-high monolith of a brown Christ. The colors, sounds, and magical quality of the yearly rituals were not so unlike those within the walls of St. Patrick's Cathedral, where Sonny spent much time in prayer and where he fed his imagination with stories from the Bible. The thick cloud of Catholic melancholy and suffering that permeated the church appealed to Sonny's own sense of estrangement and sadness. Its anguish resonated with his own. One day, however, Sonny came home from serving as head altar boy and announced that he would never again attend mass or practice the sacraments—ever. Though the particulars of the incident are lost—only Islas and the priest knew the exact details—something happened to turn him away from the church for nearly his entire life; he returned only as an adult and recovering alcoholic. Something happened that committed his "soul to eternal damnation" (Flannery O'Connor lecture). We can surmise that some form of abuse—probably sexual—took place.

Even before this break with the church, Sonny had already begun to feel alienated by religion. Later in life he would come to view the Catholic Church as an institution that only stressed "the darker side of ourselves, painted Hell in lurid colors and led us to believe that the only way we could be saved was to be as perfect as Jesus Christ" (Flannery O'Connor lecture). And religion in general began to appear weighed down in dark hypocrisy. As Sonny grew into his teens, he found in both home and the church something he called a "spiritual totalitarianism of the soul" that advocated destructive dichotomies (saint/sinner, victim/martyr) and that filled him with guilt and shame. When he was a little boy, one of the maids, María Ramírez, converted to the Seventh Day Adventist faith and began to scare him with stories to the effect that sensual pleasure was a sin against Jesus Christ and an offense that would lead to Armageddon. Islas later fictionalized this episode in his novel *The Rain God.*

An acute sense of the body's shame and sinfulness only intensified Sonny's impression that his mother was a saint and his father a sinner. On some evenings when he did his homework while his mother talked and did chores in the background, he would become overwhelmed by the feeling that she was saintly and that she gave her body to the father only so he could satisfy his shameless and beastly desire. Many years later, Islas recollected that as a child he loathed her for being "somehow sexually bound to a creature less than she (my father)" (journal, January 18, 1977). The father as sinner and mother as saint was a deeply rooted notion to which Islas returned to again and again, not just in his journals but also in his fiction. In "American Dreams and Fantasies," he fictionalized those occasions when he heard his father sexually accost his mother: "I dared not open my eyes. My heart was pounding and I was aroused by their actions while shame stole into my bed" (box 12, folder 3). The body was a site of guilt, shame, and even grief throughout Sonny's childhood and adolescence. Thoughts of his mother's body as spirit incarnate contrasted sharply with his awareness of that body's sinful penetrations by his father, and these thoughts began to shape his way of seeing his body and the world. Only much later in his life, during his twelve-step alcohol recovery program, could he finally "appreciate (without being harmed by) the very fundamental doctrines of sin and redemption and judgment which any Christian worthy of the name must believe in" (Flannery O'Connor lecture).

Even though religious doctrine—whether Seventh Day Adventist or Catholic—troubled Sonny as a child and adolescent, all was not grief and melancholy for him. Occasionally, he sought refuge from family and the scorching summer heat in a cool local movie house like El Colón, where he would watch serialized episodes of Westerns, the "glamour girl musicals," and the newsreels that taught him of worldly events ("American Dreams"). On occasion the cool interiors would also heat up, the imaginary space opening into a very immediate and tangibly dangerous reality for Islas, who recalls that "before and after the main feature . . . my cousins and I sat in awe as we watched World War II in the newsreels. We sensed *that* was real and feared that the bombs were only a few miles away. The voice of the commentator became the voice of God to us" ("American Dreams"). Also, like many other children, Sonny dreamed of being a big movie star. And, when a small company arrived in El Paso to screen child actors "for the big time," Islas "conned and begged" his

mother to give him the "ten dollar deposit" the company required to au-
dition. However, once the father learned that Jovita had indulged the
son's fantasy, yet another scene of violence ensued. Sonny never experi-
enced the fun of auditioning and instead his hopes turned to "tears, anger,
and shame" (conversation with Stina, summer 1976; box 2, folder 1).

Junior high and especially high school offered Sonny institutionally
sanctioned activities that would allow him to spend more time away
from home. El Paso High became the space in which Sonny would decide
how he wanted to experience and transform a world determined less by
parents and more by himself. He used his intelligence, good looks, and
charm to transform himself into the high school's "golden boy" (inter-
view with El Paso high school graduate Mimi Gladstein). Islas "projected
a scholarly intensity and ease of manner," recalls another classmate
(Villescas 2000, 13A), and these qualities helped pave the way for him to
become the second Mexican American in the history of the school to
serve as president of the student council—and its first Mexican American
valedictorian. He pursued academic and extracurricular activities with
the same intensity he had once felt for church, appearing in high school
parades that placed him in the limelight (once costumed as a tiger, the
school mascot). He also played in the school band. As president of
the high school student council, he was in charge of organizing all the
school's social events. School dances were a favorite of his; like his
mother, Islas loved to dance, and at these socials, he would dazzle with
his jitterbug and bunny-hop moves.

When he danced, Sonny's postpolio limp magically disappeared, and
high school was also all about mobility and choice. That he was one of few
teenagers to own a car—a 1948 Chevy hand-me-down—added not just to
his freedom but also to his popularity. This sense of self-determination
spilled over into his home life. His father built a bedroom for Sonny at the
back of the family's house on Almagordo Street, so he would no longer
have to share a room with his two younger brothers. Here and at school
he began to carve out a life for himself away from family and on his own
terms.

Sonny re-formed himself into an individual at the center and not the
margins of the academic and social scene—the place that his polio limp

and the era's rampant ethnic discrimination would "normally" assign him. He was a performer. He was also unwilling to reveal his "real" self for fear of being hurt and was deeply insecure about his academic ability; and though he managed to hide the fact of his faulty body at school dances, a deep sense of ugliness lingered. He felt lost and alone. Sonny, as the adult writer Islas fictionalizes in *Migrant Souls*, "was one of the loneliest people in the world" (1990b, 67). (Later, feeling compelled to perform the role of a "straight" professor in the classroom and in front of homophobic colleagues, he felt equally alone.) And, his self-determined space at the back of the house helped him escape family problems but didn't make them disappear. He often woke up to overhear fights between his mother and father that would leave him doubled over with stomach pains. He reframes the experience in *Migrant Souls:* "From the kitchen, the voices of his mother and father broke like chimes into his reveries and the knot in his chest tightened. The morning demons were wrapping barbed wire around his heart" (175). For all of the new liberties and opportunities high school life offered, Sonny went on trying to disentangle knots of sadness and anger—the father's tyranny and the mother's martyrdom—that affected him viscerally.

MATERFAMILIAS

Sonny identified himself mostly with his mother's melancholy sensibility and her victimhood, whereas Jovita looked to him as a confidant. When the sounds of his father's (mostly) verbal abuse of his mother seeped at night through Sonny's bedroom walls, his sympathies were clearly for the "victim." The bond of victimhood between mother and son was already in place when the eight-year-old Sonny fell ill. Instead of challenging Arturo Sr.'s harsh response to her own suggestion that Sonny needed a doctor—"I'm head of this family, and you're not calling anybody. I won't have you spoil him anymore. You've already taken him away from me"—Jovita stood by and watched her son suffer ("Día"; box 5, folder 4). As Sonny's condition worsened, his father's denial deepened and so too did the bond between mother and son. Arturo Sr. perceived

this, Islas writes, as "their intricately woven web of feeling for one an-
other" ("Día"). And the disease only exacerbated the struggle between
son and father for Jovita's affections; it caused a breach between Sonny
and Arturo Sr. that never healed.

Poliomyelitis marked the point when Islas consciously turned from
his father's emotional cold-shouldering and toward his mother. Years
later, when Islas returned to El Paso from California for the summer in
1967, his anger toward and alienation from his father hit another critical
juncture. He discovered his father's love affair with Jovita's close friend.
He also recognized that his mother, who blamed herself, played the mar-
tyr role to a self-destructive degree. She had known about the affair for
over three years, he discovered, but did nothing. Finally, when it was
made public—and not through Jovita's active intervention—she felt
more guilty than outraged. She felt responsible for the affair, responsible
because she was not as beautiful as her friend—who had those physical
qualities Arturo Sr. thought sexy and that Jovita thought would have
kept him happy and at home if only she possessed them. In a letter to
Islas she writes, "I had failed him so miserably as he has tried to tell me
and explain to me" (December 1, 1967). What angered him was not only
the tyrant/victim cycles that continued at home throughout his life, but
the apparently conscious replication of saint/sinner, asexual/sexual, and
spirit/body dualities, with virgin/whore dialectics as part of the trian-
gle. By playing the martyr role, his mother was repeating age-old codes
of behavior—the mother of Arturo Sr.'s children and hence a figure not
invested in bodily pleasure—that upheld gendered oppression. Thus, in
a letter to Islas, his father depicted his mother as saintly and the mother
of his children, and his mistress as all body and the only one, he writes,
"that can halfway satisfy my sex urge" (January 16, 1968). Islas would
later write of the morning his father left his mother for a trip to Califor-
nia with his mistress and how Jovita responded only with silence, iron-
ing "two of his better dress shirts" and repacking his suitcase ("Día").
Taking up the father/tyrant role, the adult Islas wrote a letter to his
mother that expressed his rage at her passive-aggressive behavior, read-
ing it as a form of manipulation of the father. Whether manipulated or
not, Arturo Sr. returned home after his trip. So, as family friend Earl

Shorris remarks of their breakup, "The toughest cop the town had ever known never considered leaving his wife, for he treasured her and his family" (1992, 435). When her husband came home, Jovita wrote Sonny: "I am happy and my job now is to make him happy because he is really all that I have" (July 23, 1970).

As an adult, Islas gained insight into how his parents' tyrant/victim behavioral patterns were replicated in his own relationships. Islas was fully aware of his identification with the martyr role in his obsessive love for an emotionally abusive and tyrannical Jay Spears. At one point, he even asks himself in a journal entry: "How much have Jay and my mother collaborated in this way of seeing myself?" (January 18, 1977). During his relationship with Spears, Islas would often endure night-mares of Jay acting tyrannically and his mother dying. He also dreamed that he was unable to move because he was paralyzed, like his mother, as a "beautiful zombie" and yet "ankle deep . . . in shit" (July 9, 1984). Islas's alter ego played out his wish for action and yet Islas himself re-mained, like his mother, immobilized by self-pity.

As he recognized his parents' relationship in his own dysfunctional re-playing of their dynamics, the adult Islas began to see his home in a dif-ferent light. He saw "the strengths and weaknesses parents give to their children so freely—without counting the costs, one of them being an un-bearable sadness at leaving. Mother = nervous anticipation about every-thing that needs to be done (and which will never get done, will have to be done again and again like cleaning the house) / Joy, Innocence, Danc-ing. Father = lying and insisting on the lie / Fantasy, Protector, a Cactus. Ha!" (August 10, 1987). However, these equations failed to tell the whole story. Islas felt time and again the need to go beyond them. Thus, in an-other dream sequence, he morphs into an orphan and finds himself, he writes in his journal,

in strange/familiar places with many people floating in and out of the dream. My parents have disowned me—first my father, then my mother. I am orphaned, sad, not zombieland, but dull perpetual anxiety *that is there,* not strong enough to incapacitate, dim enough to be felt. I walk and act in spite of it. Whose child am I, then? Somewhere in a house a tele-phone rings. I answer. The woman's voice on the other end says, "I am your real mother," in an emotionally charged tone. I am simultaneously moved by curiosity and fear, a feeling of "I-knew-all-along-I-did-not-belong-to-these-people." Now I'm going to meet my real mother. We arrange to meet. By the end of the dream, I am still waiting for her. I didn't even ask her name. (box 53, folder 3, January 18, 1977)

PATERFAMILIAS

As I mentioned earlier, Islas's early identification with his mother grew largely out of his rejection of his father's macho codes of conduct. He felt oppressed by his father's emotional distance and moody silences; he was also overwhelmed by his father's strong physical presence—one he could never aspire to possess because of his postpolio limp and later his colostomy. The fact that Sonny could not be the jock-son his father wanted to carry on the Islas line estranged father from son. Whenever there was physical contact between the two, Islas recounts in the auto-biographical "Día de los muertos," "it was limited to a slap in the face or a bone crushing *abrazo* that lacked affection." His father's hugs and other patently macho expressions were meant to show the son that he was physically stronger and more fit. Islas powerfully sublimated his feelings of estrangement from his father, dreaming on one occasion as an adult how, he writes in his journal, "My father comes in the back door of the old house. Behind him, the landscape is frozen in snow and ice. He looks young, lean and brown, is carrying a bicycle" (October 23, 1976). Throughout Islas's life, the father symbolized that strong physicality and cold emotional state that he could never embody. So he became his father's opposite: an individual committed to the life of the mind.

Islas turned to books and scholarly achievement both to come to terms with his father's affectless touch and to gain the respect and affection of his father in spite of his postpolio disability. But because of his limp, he would never find respect in his father's eyes; this awareness became even more painfully obvious to Islas when his youngest brother, Louie, grew into the jock the father always wanted as a son. His father lavished attention and macho-coded affection on Louie and sidelined Islas. This is not to say that Islas did not eventually gain some respect from his father.

At last, when Islas had nearly earned his PhD, his father sent him a letter dated January 16, 1968: "I cannot possibly let you know how proud I am of your accomplishments and how much it does to my ego, when I tell all the people of you teaching at Stanford." The father's expression of pride in Islas's achievement seemed long overdue and yet, Islas still feared, it simply masked deeper insecurities—and jealousies—in relation to his son's accomplishments. In an undated note, he remarked that his father was "an unhappy man whose sense of inferiority is equal only to the force of his denial of that sense" (box 2, folder 1).

Around the same time, Islas became aware that he desired only men; if his father found out about his gay sexuality, he knew he would disown him. After all, Islas knew of his father's loathing for the *joto* (fag). It was also during this period that Islas wrestled with his conflicting emotions over his father's affair. Islas began to channel his feelings for his father into patricidal fantasies. Regarding one such dreamscape fantasy, he writes in his journal, "My father is dead. My brothers and I take a city bus to the morgue which is across from the Catholic hospital. Both Mario and Louie have seen my father's corpse already and refuse to stay" (August 17, 1967; box 53, folder 3). In another dreamscape, Islas sees himself splitting into two: an adult who witnesses his father and mother struggling not to sink "to the bottom of a lake [by] holding on to the side of a skiff [and a child-self that] no one makes an effort to save," and a child witnessing himself drown and "then slowly rise to the surface" (January 4, 1977; box 53, folder 3). In therapy sessions during the mid-1960s, Islas tried to talk through these dreams and come to terms with his love/hate relationship with his father—a relationship he knew was dysfunctional but that he could not cut out of his life.

The adult Islas knew by experience that he too was capable of playing either victim or tyrant. He describes in his journal on February 24, 1987, "how my father's rage has affected me. How terrified of it I was as a child of him." He did not want to become the violent and *machista* person his father was. In "American Dreams and Fantasies," the protagonist reflects how he needs to "keep constant watch over that part of me that is in any way like him." Much of the fiction Islas wrote during this period was an attempt to become conscious of and keep at bay any expression of his father's destructive behavior. He used autobiographical fiction as a means to explore unconscious human behavior within a larger context. His thinly veiled self-as-narrator remarks of his father, "What interests me most about him in relation to all these elusive myths is how notions of *machismo* merged in him with the notions of masculinity" ("American Dreams"). Moving away from the father who erupted in misogynistic bursts of temper ("Women are shit, you know that?" the fictionalized father says in "Día") with the help of his fiction and of his therapy sessions with Dr. Paulsen, Islas learned to control his own violent behavior. In the same letter in which he portrays Jovita as a saintly mother, his father wrote that he not only felt emotionally worn out over his affair and his leaving Jovita, but also felt quite inadequate as a father (January 16, 1968; box 53, folder 2). In unguarded terms that somewhat surprised Islas, the elder Islas admitted in later correspondence that he had leaned on his son and channeled his feelings of "love and dependency" away from the mother onto the son (November 30, 1968; box 53, folder 2). But Islas was tired of his father's words and skeptical: was this honesty or simply another way to manipulate and keep his hold over the family? In Islas's reply, he told his father not to confess unless he was going to recognize his destructive behavior; he told him not to cry on his son's shoulder just to massage his own ego. And as Islas had predicted, as soon as the father's crisis subsided and Jovita took him back into the nest, he reverted to his usual—abusive or distant behavior toward the son and the mother. Afterward, Islas received only polite, emotionally distant letters from his father. Islas responded in kind, with polite, unemotional letters—even during the time when he was most upset and had turned to alcohol—when he discovered that his partner had been indulging in S&M for some time with another man and wanted to leave Islas. Though he regretted that he could not share with his emotions with his father—"Dad, Jay doesn't want me," he writes to himself in his journal on November 8, 1978—he knew that his father would never reciprocate, would never understand, and would only further distance himself (box 53, folder 3).

Therapy sessions with Dr. Paulsen, as well as journal entries, poetry, and autobiographical fiction, provided Islas with a means to understand himself by redirecting the strong currents of emotion that flowed in through the paternal line. In his journal entries—that domain ordinarily considered the most private, and therefore the most factual—Islas manipulated characters he invented to help him understand his father. In one such entry, he writes, "In my crazy thought, I begin to see that Beto [his imaginary older brother] was his first son and that he considered me a spoiled brat—and still does" (August 22, 1988; box 55, folder 1). In fiction he displaced his very real anger away from his father and onto the characters he invented. As a result, Islas records in his journals, his father "has never known what to make of me. I was the brilliant 'brat' he sought to put down at every turn. Never has he praised any of my accomplishments, always has he sensed I was 'different.' He does not like me. But you know what? *I do not like him.* How freeing to know that, how freeing *not* to want/need his approval. *That* has been killing me" (December 26, 1988). Fictionalized fact and therapy sessions had a common goal: "to annihilate whatever I see of my father in myself" (February 24, 1987).

FRATERNITY

While the mother and father were central in the formation of certain patterns that Arturo Islas struggled to understand and overcome, his two younger brothers, Mario Guillermo and Luis Eduardo, also exerted a powerful influence in his life. They grew up under the same roof and formative parental dynamics, though each experienced the family differently. Reflecting on his brothers, Islas writes, "In the tradition of the masculine ethic that sees the overcoming of obstacles as the only way to make a man out of a boy, my father has made life difficult for his three sons" (note; box 2, folder 1). Mario, four years younger than Islas, sought refuge in the church instead of the university. The youngest, Luis, embraced the father's macho codes, excelling in sports and cultivating a bad-boy public persona. In a sense, each developed his own individual coping and escape mechanism. As Islas sums up: "My middle brother escaped into the church. My youngest brother, most loved by my father, has become like him. I fled into academia. Bad fathers (are there any other kind?) make good students" (note; box 2, folder 1).

Luis, with his athletic predisposition, easily won his father's favor. He was the chubby little brother who grew into a strappingly good-looking, athletic high school jock. The father made sure he had every athletic opportunity available as a teenager, fashioning him into the son he always wanted. In Islas's eyes, Louie (as he was called) embraced his father's agenda wholeheartedly, becoming El Paso High's star athlete and, following closely in the father's footsteps, ever more popular with the girls. Though Islas was far away at Stanford, Louie's success in the eyes of the father only reminded him of his own deficiencies as a son. When Louie won a college football scholarship to attend Stanford, the father expressed his wholehearted delight, which he hadn't done when Islas won an academic scholarship several years earlier to the same school. When Louie left home for Stanford in 1967, the father let Islas know that he could not fill the void Louie left in his life when he went away to school. The father also publicly declared, during holiday family gatherings, that Louie shared his manly good looks and self-confidence in the company of women. Islas too shared his father's good looks, but what looked like a lack of success with women—and a physical disability—made him vastly inferior to Louie in his father's eyes.

In spite of this, Arturo and Louie were very close. The older brother often played the mentor to Louie, introducing him to different rock bands he'd heard and, as a Stanford graduate student, advising Louie on how to study. Also, when Louie confided in him about relationship problems, he pointed out ways to cope with Stanford's academic challenges. More significantly, on occasion Louie communicated a not so self-assured side of his personality to Islas, writing, "I am not a happy teenager in High School" (April 27, 1965; box 1, folder 11). And in an earlier letter, he related his grief over the "unforgivable way" their gay uncle, Carlos (Arturo Sr.'s brother), was murdered: "I was not shocked at it. It surprised me, but with all that I know that is going on in the world today I can accept it. I feel that there is no crime worst than taking a life and if the other man's statement on Carlos's actions is true, it is still nothing compared to murder. I would like to know what went on that night, but I will never know" (March 22, 1965). Seeing his younger brother's expression of a sensitivity toward the world's injustices, Islas was prompt and eager to act as guide and mentor to Louie.

At Stanford, Louie and Islas spent more time together than they had spent while at home—and their bond strengthened. Islas's abhorrence of Louie's hyper-macho swagger dissipated somewhat as he became more aware of the depth of Louie's own pain and suffering. And Louie would be the first person in the family to learn that Islas was gay; later he often visited Islas and his partner, Edward Bergh, at their rented house in Palo Alto. Also, some time later, when Louie had started Stanford's law program, he introduced to his older brother to the man who would become Islas's great love, Jay Spears.

Islas's relationship with his brother Mario remained uneven throughout their lives. Islas loved and was loved by Mario but always considered himself superior to him. He deemed the world Mario entered to be of a lower intellectual rank than the ones Louie and he himself chose: Mario studied to become a priest, not a lawyer or a professor. And then Mario was second in the order of birth. As children and then as teenagers, Islas tyrannized Mario. Associating him with the mother and identifying with the father, Islas put Mario down for not being as smart and successful. The older brother would not tolerate even the most minor offense on Mario's part. During meals, Islas would give Mario "dirty looks," showing a disgust for his eating habits and posture. Islas would remind Mario constantly of how he was ashamed to be his brother because he was so slow to learn. When Islas was older he saw that this behavior had been a means of deflecting the feelings of shame and insecurity he had acquired in his relationship with their father, but it entrenched the differences between the brothers. When Mario entered El Paso High, constant reminders from teachers of the older brother's brilliance broadened the gap between them. Mario sums up the experience in a letter he sent to Islas much later in life:

[You] certainly were a hard act to follow. Being your younger brother was *not* easy. The way I saw it was you were perfect. The perfect student, the perfect friend, everything about you was perfect. I tried like hell to be just like you. But I failed miserably—so I thought. You were so perfect and everything fell into place for you so well and I wanted that. I can remember even signing up for some of the same classes and teachers you had in high school. Suffice it to say—I wanted to be like you and I tried very hard to do just that. (February 6, 1990; box 4, folder 6)

The divide between them widened further when Mario chose to leave El Paso to study to become a priest. Islas rejected the institution his younger brother chose to embrace. But clearly for Mario, the decision was a way to claim a space Islas had not already colonized, so to speak. Successful as a priest, Mario became less "obsessed" (his word) with wanting to be like Islas. He was able to stand his ground, asking at one point when they were adults that Islas accept him on his own terms, to establish a more equal relationship. This came about when Mario confided to his older brother feelings of alienation as a gay man and Islas in turn mentioned his troubled love for Jay Spears. In 1978, desperate, Islas wrote to Mario, "People like us cannot be happy in the world because the world is against us from the very beginning. Not because of any intrinsic desire on our part to be unhappy, but because the world is simply repelled by the idea of two people of the same sex (especially two men) expressing their love for each other. It will take a long, long time to change the world's attitude and it certainly won't happen in my life time. I despair" (February 12, 1978; box 3, folder 6). By sharing their secrets, Mario wrote to Islas, they became equals, neither one "superior or inferior" to the other (February 6, 1990; box 4, folder 6).

Unfortunately, the occupation that gave Mario a sense of purpose and confidence in his dealings with the world was taken from him, according to the family, when the church used him as a scapegoat. For five years, Mario had given money and food to a homeless heroin addict within the San Elizario parish in El Paso. In a sensational account, the *El Paso Times* reported that Mario had received sexual favors from this homeless man. On March 5, 1987, Islas reflects in his journal: "How carelessly, how casually, how cruelly these people seek to destroy lives. It's on the radio, the T.V., both papers" (box 55, folder 1). Allegations that a priest had used embezzled funds to pay for sexual favors were never proved, but Mario was banished from his El Paso parish. (The family considers the charges an act of news myth-making, the result of half-baked investigative reporting and allegation from unidentified sources.) The bishop quietly asked Mario to leave for Hartford, Connecticut, where he underwent therapy at a Catholic institute. Mario had suddenly fallen from grace and thus from his father's regard. Arturo Sr. was infuriated that the scandal would tarnish his reputation and stigmatize him as the father of a "perverted" son. According to Islas's recollection, the father told his friends how "Mario fucked up and is evaluating his vocation" (journal, December 23, 1987; box 55, folder 1). Islas was angry that Mario would not put up a fight, but sympathized deeply with Mario and his predicament.

MATRIX

Islas came to see his family as martyrs and tyrants, saints and sinners, all informing his sense of self in and beyond his home in El Paso. At times he raged against his father—and struggled to break free from his hostility throughout his life. At different moments he had to fight both against the victim role he associated with his mother and brother Mario and against the tyrant role he associated with his father and his partner, Jay Spears. Such internal conflicts plagued Islas, often manifesting themselves in self-destructive acts, deep depressions, and suicidal tendencies. He registered wild swings of emotion every day—anger then sadness, exhilaration then depression, anxiety, and paranoia. He notes one such swing: "I AM IN GRAND SPIRITS. . . . How am I getting through these days? A vague discontent; premonitions of disaster" (February 13, 1983; box 54, folder 6). Throughout his life he endured restless nights, often waking up in tears. Though he tried to escape by drinking and taking drugs, he realized they only made his mood swings more extreme. Continual therapy and a stay in an AA clinic eventually helped him acknowledge the past that continued to live in his present.

Islas kept up a performance of perfection. There were no visible cracks in his glossy veneer. He was a successful and respected professor at Stanford University who won accolades and prizes; he was the pillar of support and a confidant to friends and family. He had learned the father's lesson well: never reveal your weakness. Behind the performance was a deeply conflicted and emotionally scarred man. He was profoundly insecure and obsessed with how others regarded him. He sought approval at home and at school, as a writer and as a professor.

Even so, in Islas's emotional landscape, his family and home in El Paso existed not only as a site of trauma, but also as a place of healing. In spite of all the family dysfunction, he loved his parents and brothers deeply. Like the desert he loved as a child and returned to as an adult, both in fiction and in his travels, home was treacherous and barren but also held the promise of life. For Islas, home was a place where anger mixed with love, fear with desire, death with life. It embodied these disparate forces—desert sun and electric rain—and offered a refuge from a world that sought to restrict and schematize his sense of self in the world. No matter where he was situated, he returned to that desertscape of his childhood where no categories would restrict subjectivity because, as he writes in his prose poem "Cuauhtémoc's Grave," "it is nameless there, anonymous, alienated" (box 9, folder 5). Not surprisingly, before Islas died in February 1991, he asked that half of his ashes be scattered in the desert of West Texas so that he might return home and rest in peace.

TWO Bio-Graphé

The hard-won publication of his novel *The Rain God* in 1984 secured Arturo Islas a significant place in the field of Chicano/a letters. Today, *The Rain God* appears in the syllabi of colleges and even high schools across the nation. Of course, there is much more to Islas than *The Rain God*. There are his other novels: the boldly poetic, darkly complex sequel, *Migrant Souls* (mystifyingly out of print), and his *La Mollie and the King of Tears* (published posthumously). As far back as his undergraduate creative writing days at Stanford in the late 1950s, Islas was making visible a multiplicity of Chicano/a voices, experiences, and visions in his short stories, poetry, and beautifully crafted letters.[1]

A central motif in Arturo Islas's work is that of recovery. Often his deserts recover bodies and voices as wind-whipped sands sweep across high-desert Del Sapo (his fictionalized El Paso) and the U.S./Mexico bor-

derland plains. His sands cover over such bodies and voices—and re-
cover or uncover and make visible others. The act of reading Islas
through his writing is an act of recovering a complex individual. Islas's
writing not only cycles through acts of re-covering (making disappear)
and recovering (making appear by narrating, remembering, and forget-
ting) but also speaks to those Chicano/a subjects that inhabit a constant
state of "recovery" and longing for health and life in a society permeated
by racism and by heterosexism in two forms, Euro-American and Chi-
cano—neither of which is hospitable to the gay or lesbian Chicano/a.

The act of recovery was not just a clever literary trope for Islas. As a
Chicano teaching the first Chicanas/os at Stanford University in the late
1960s and early 1970s, he knew that there was much to be recovered and
discovered in Chicano/a textual productions. He looked to his students'
creative writing as one such site of literary recovery. By 1970 there were
nearly two hundred Chicanos enrolled at Stanford: seventy freshman,
twenty transfer students, and nearly forty graduate students. During the
early 1970s, Islas encouraged his students to write narratives about the
Chicano/a experience. As time passed, he amassed a sizable collection of
their short stories, prose poems, and literary essays.

He called these first-generation Stanford undergraduates his "pio-
neers," applauding their dedication to making visible Chicano/a cre-
ative expression and their struggle against institutional and individual
racist acts. Islas described his course as giving "Chicano upperclassmen
the opportunity to read and write about the literature that derives from
their own background. It will also provide students the opportunity to
write fiction and poetry which draws from their Chicano heritage and ex-
perience. There is a dearth of literature from the Spanish-speaking cul-
ture in this country. Its particular language is rich in possibilities and has
been explored only recently by contemporary poets Alurista and Omar
Salinas" (Chicano literature lecture; box 33, folder 1).

The 1974 publication of a journal Islas pushed hard to establish,
Miquiztli: A Journal of Arte, Poesía, Cuento, y Canto, marked a moment at
Stanford when people were ready to pay attention to Chicano/a creative
expression. The journal's focus was the U.S./Mexican borderland space,
where culture, history, and racial identities and experience would inter-

sect. In the inaugural issue, Islas's introduction identified this as the journal that would give voice to "the fact of our double heritage" and that would provide the venue for Chicano/a literary expression for an "audience interested enough to understand and appreciate it" (box 6, folder 12). Its multiple junctures—not unlike Islas's multiracial El Paso—framed a less parochial understanding of the world. *Miquiztli* marked a significant moment in the rise of Chicano/a literary studies at Stanford, for it gave Islas and his students a way to articulate the vast spectrum of Chicano/a experiences through poetry and prose, short story and autobiography. It introduced poetry by José David Saldívar, one of Islas's first Chicano PhD students, and by the writer Bernice Zamora. Significantly, Islas believed that a writer's work merited treatment as literature only if it held up to an evaluation based on form and content. In the second volume of *Miquiztli* (1975), for example, Islas writes, "More often than not, much of the fiction we do have is document, and sometimes not very well written document. Much of what is passed off as literature is a compendium of folklore, religious superstition, and recipes for tortillas. All well and good, but it is not literature" (box 6, folder 11). Both journal and classroom gave Islas a forum to recover an array of Chicano/a textual voices and experiences.

Islas also pushed to "legitimate" Chicano studies by teaming up with young Chicano professors like historian Al Camarillo, anthropologist Renato Rosaldo, and cultural critic Tomás Ybarra-Frausto. Together, they organized and team-taught courses (for example, the "Interdisciplinary Research Seminar on Chicano Culture"), including on the syllabus titles like Ron Arias's *Road to Tamazunchale*, Charles Tatum's *Chicano Literature*, and Francisco Jiménez's *Identification and Analysis of Chicano Literature*. Whether as part of a team or alone, Islas's lectures were both laudatory and critical of Chicano/a literature. He had been trained to judge literary texts according to their formal qualities and how effectively they reflected and commented on the "real" social landscape beyond the text. For example, in a lecture on Ernesto Galarza's *Education of a Barrio Boy*, he discussed both the book's importance as a retelling of Galarza's life as a migrant farmworker and its lack of narrative subtlety and stylistic polish. Islas would tell his students to develop a discerning readerly taste that would appreciate not only a book's content but also its form—in this case, Galarza's lack of nuance and storytelling craft. Furthermore, Islas was careful to distinguish between Chicano writers who were able to tell complex stories of the Chicano self in society and those who, like Galarza, produced a one-dimensional portrait of the Chicano struggling to survive in the United States. Later, with the popularity of minority studies on the rise, he continued to team-teach but also taught his own courses, choosing for them subjects that went beyond the Chicano authors. Thus, he taught courses like "Hispanic American Novels," where, according to his own description, students "will read and discuss works by some of the major contemporary Hispanic American writers," and he expanded the Chicano/a literary canon to include Latino writers such as Gabriel García Márquez *(One Hundred Years of Solitude)*, Mario Vargas Llosa *(Aunt Julia and the Scriptwriter)*, Carlos Fuentes *(The Good Conscience)*, and Juan Rulfo *(Pedro Páramo* and *The Burning Plain)*.

Islas's role as professor did not begin and end with students in the classroom. Along with Camarillo, Rosaldo, and Ybarra-Frausto, he made sure that his Chicano/a students had institutional support to research and write on Chicano/a topics. One of his students, José Jesús Cazares, wrote a paper titled "The Totality of Male Domination vs. Sexual Pleasure: Homosexuality in Chicano Literature," and another, Inés Salazar, wrote a paper titled "La Frontera and the Cyborg: Possibilities for the Creation of Alternative Spaces." With Islas's guidance and Stanford's institutional support, both wrote papers that were far ahead of their day. Such research support was formally established as the Chicano Fellows Program in 1971; and in 1980—after years of pounding on administrators' doors—Islas, Camarillo, Rosaldo, and Ybarra-Frausto were granted their own space on the campus and formed the Chicano Research Center. (Today, this is known as the Center for the Studies of Race and Ethnicity.) So, though Islas considered himself more of a creative writer than researcher, he valued scholarly production as another form of legitimating, in the eyes of the mainstream, Chicano/a cultural production. Islas recalled the initial impulse of the Chicano Fellows Program at an alumni conference in Los Angeles, remarking how the program sought to make visible "the Chicano imagination and point of view" not just to Chicanas/os, but to "include as many students as are interested."

As the new (mostly male) Chicano voices emerged in the new literary landscape—Oscar "Zeta" Acosta, Rudolfo Anaya, Ron Arias, Raymond Barrio, Ernesto Galarza, Rolando Hinojosa, Tomás Rivera, Antonio Villarreal, Víctor Villaseñor, Alurista, and José Montoya—scholarly production also received support and continued to develop.

In 1975, with *Miquiztli*, Chicano/a literature courses peppering the curriculum, and the Chicano Fellows Program well under way, Islas turned his focus to writing the seventy-page scholarly monograph titled "Saints, Artists, and Vile Politics: An Introduction to Chicano Fiction and Autobiography" (box 15, folder 3). The project as a whole both engaged and critiqued the "uneasy relationship" (his words) between Latin American and Anglo literatures. While many of his colleagues at Stanford praised the project, Islas never found any interest among the academic presses. In "Saints," Islas combined an Yvor Wintersian analysis (close reading combined with a candid, subjective judgment) with a racialized edge to read a variety of Chicano writers, among them Oscar "Zeta" Acosta, Rudolfo A. Anaya, Ernesto Galarza, and Rolando Hinojosa, along with some Latin American authors, such as Gabriel García Márquez. In a study far ahead of its time, Islas not only constructed a North and South American literary frame of analysis, but also articulated an intricate method for reading Chicano literature that paid attention both to its poetics and its themes. "Saints" critiqued traditional studies of American literature, which typically followed an East-to-West critical gaze (with the "real" writers largely inhabiting the East), by analyzing how Chicano/a literature existed along a North-South continuum of genre influence and exchange. Islas also dared to use the autobiographical voice to shed a different light on his primary texts—this during a time before the multicultural confessional voice had become a legitimate mode of scholarly critique in the academy. For example, in his discussion of *Barrio Boy*, Islas concludes, "I consider myself, still, a child of the Border, a Border some believe extends all the way to Seattle and includes the northern provinces of Mexico. . . . Like some of my characters, I often find myself on the bridge between cultures, between languages, between sexes, between nations, between religions, between my profession as teacher and my vocation as writer, between two different and equally compelling ways of looking agape at the world" (box 30, folder 11). Islas sought to construct theoretical bridges that were anchored strongly in the autobiographical. He thus attempted in his scholarly work on Chicano/a literature to clear a space where he could develop a comparative analytic approach that was also grounded in the personal. He sought to think and write across disciplines (scholarly and personal) as if walking, as he wrote in "Saints," "from one side of the border to another without any immigration officers to tell me where I should or should not be" (box 30, folder 11).

Islas came of age as a Chicano writer and scholar during a splitting in the way literature was to be studied in the U.S. academy: between a traditional belletristic appreciation of literature and the new wave of French theory, which questioned universal truths and structures and deconstructed the text. Islas found himself stuck between the two: pulled by his training under the guidance of Stanford's belletrists, Wallace Stegner, Ian Watt, David Levin, Thomas Moser, and Yvor Winters, but also pulled by the new French approaches to scholarship, which spoke to issues of Otherness and that sought to destabilize traditional paradigms that read Europe as the literary center and the Americas as peripheral. Islas cleared a space that was informed by both methods of approaching the literary text—be it Chicano/a or Anglo-American.

His finding of a balance between literary appreciation and a deconstructive and politicized reading of the text began with his dissertation, "The Work of Hortense Callisher: On Middle Ground" (box 16, folder 1), which he completed in 1971, just as his interest in Chicano/a literature was beginning to take shape. His approach was innovative in several respects. He analyzed Callisher's work—a marginal figure in American literary studies at the time—within a cultural and social context. He intentionally chose this marginal literary figure, and he also intentionally chose a writer who was still living. As Islas noted in an interview with José Antonio Burciaga, in those days, the subjects of dissertations "had to be dead, at least fifty years!" (November 28, 1990; box 2, folder 1). Wallace Stegner, his principal advisor, "was breaking an unwritten rule," Islas told Burciaga, in agreeing to Islas's project. Stegner may have approved because he knew Callisher; he had invited her to teach at Stan-

ford when Islas was a sophomore, and it was while attending her gradu-
ate seminar that Islas was first introduced to her work—work that had a
lasting impression. Islas chose Callisher as the subject of his study, how-
ever, not just because of the personal contact, but because he could tease
out of her works her nuanced interweaving of politics and aesthetics.
Also, he chose Callisher because, at the time, she made central tradition-
ally taboo or marginal areas of study in English literary analysis: gender
and racial Otherness. In an analysis of her Jewish female characters, Islas
writes how they exist in between a "rooted and rootless" identity and ex-
perience of the world ("Callisher"). He also distinguishes Callisher from
Saul Bellow, Bernard Malamud, and Philip Roth, who portray their Jew-
ish characters as suffering from a more general alienation as human be-
ings, and not because "they are Jews." For Islas, then, Callisher is able to
create racialized and gendered characters who experience the world in a
certain way that is colored by their particular marginal positions (he fo-
cuses especially on Callisher's Jewish character Hester). At the same
time, however, she complicates them by making them "unique because
they are different from others as people and not exclusively because they
are Jews." Callisher herself, in a 1965 essay titled "Can There Be an Amer-
ican C. P. Snow?" lauds "novelists working in beautifully polished bas-
relief, in some savagely intense corner of adolescence, homosexuality, or
racial sensibility." Islas comments that Callisher may work in one such
"intense corner," but she "is careful to get out of it and describe it from
the middle of the room as part of a broader context." Callisher's charac-
ters are not just racial, sexual, and gendered outcasts, but, as he wrote,
"neither heroic nor bizarre, which is to say that they are neither upper
nor lower class. They are in the middle and preoccupied with the ordi-
nary business of day-to-day living. In gradual, quiet ways, alone or in
pairs, they come to their insights about or make their compromises with
the City, themselves, or others" (100). Class, for Islas, as well as race and
gender, positions characters within a "middle ground" where they exist,
he writes, "in a state of in-between" (164). But Islas also appreciated Call-
isher because she fleshed out the characters' experience of childhood
pain and passion within relationships—themes that preoccupied Islas in
his own life. Finally, Islas was drawn to this author because of her status

as a liminal literary figure: she was a Jewish woman writing about women in a man's canon, and as such she was relatively invisible, considered second rate.

Islas had to take time off from writing the dissertation to recover from a series of operations—the colostomy that I discuss at length in chapter 4—and so the writing of the dissertation stretched over a longer than average period of time. With encouragement from both Hortense Callisher and Ian Watt, Islas finished the dissertation in 1971, but new literary currents would soon take him in a different direction. After the 1972 publication of the English translation of García Márquez's *One Hundred Years of Solitude* helped anchor firmly some major Latin American writers on the international literary map, Islas realized that these writers—Juan Rulfo, Jorge Luis Borges, Carlos Fuentes, Julio Cortázar, Mario Vargas Llosa, and quite a few others—had been dealing with issues of race and gender "in spades and doing it beautifully" (Burciaga interview). He put his dissertation on Callisher aside as Chicano/a and Latino/a writers became more visible. The fact that Islas wasn't interested in turning his dissertation into a book would later affect his case for tenure. Plus, the scholarship he engaged in after the dissertation was on writers no one in the department had heard of, so few knew how to appraise his work. To add to this confusion, Islas had begun to seriously pursue the writing of fiction. He had already begun writing his "Día de los muertos," the draft of a novel about a Chicano growing up in a U.S./Mexico border town and later exploring his queer sexuality in the San Francisco S&M and bathhouse scene. Islas worried about the tenure decision: "I didn't think I would be offered tenure because I wasn't writing, nor did I want to write, the kinds of things that get you tenure at a place like Stanford. I just kept writing my novels and articles about Chicano literature" (interview with Ricardo Aguilar Melantzón).

Islas did manage to secure his position as a Chicano professor and scholar, primarily because of his teaching—the element of his file Stanford English faculty knew how to evaluate. In a letter addressed to Chairman John Loftis, an anonymous outside reviewer of Islas's scholarly and fictional work concludes, "I suspect that the strength of his achievement at present shows more clearly in his efforts as a sympathetic teacher"

(November 21, 1975; box 7, folder 1). And when John Felstiner, resident Latin Americanist and translator of Pablo Neruda, was asked to evaluate Islas's tenure case, he supported Islas's scholarship and creative writing, but emphasized the teaching, commenting that Islas was "a teacher of rare gifts, in fact unique," and concluding, "I simply cannot imagine the University without his presence as a teacher" (letter, October 23, 1975; box 7, folder 1). Perhaps not such a surprising response to a Chicano professor whose scholarly and creative work was not traditional.

Islas was very adept at negotiating social borders. As an undergraduate, graduate, and professor at Stanford, he could enter and be politic in a community of mostly straight, male, Ivy-league academics, and then return to his writing and life at the canonic and social margins. Islas chose his battles carefully, working with diplomatic care to redraft and rebuild the proverbial master's house from within. He strategically mixed belletristic analysis—judging fictional narratives and poems according to the evaluative style of his undergraduate and graduate mentor, Yvor Winters—with a deconstructive zeal for the political and marginal—focusing more and more on identifying a Chicano/a aesthetic. As a Chicano writer and academic, Islas worked successfully to complicate the experiential contours of the American literary landscape while attaining employment security and intellectual prestige.

SHORT STORIES

Islas had already begun to come into a richly imagined sense of self as a late teen and young adult long before he achieved recognition from English department colleagues and mainstream publishing houses. Largely inspired by his own experiences of the Southwest (or what has been identified by Américo Paredes, Lázaro Cárdenas, and José Limón as "Greater Mexico"), Islas began to invent stories that reflected his and other Chicanos' everyday cultural, economic, and racial U.S./Mexico borderland.

Islas was born on May 25, 1938—two months after the president of Mexico, Lázaro Cárdenas, opened the border to American capitalism and nationalized Mexican oil. On the one hand, this meant that Juárez and El Paso would become more of an American/Mexican metropolis in terms of business and commerce. On the other hand, it meant that movement across the border from Mexico to the United States would increasingly be regulated so as to ensure a steady supply of "illegals" to provide the cheap labor that would build El Paso. Islas would grow up to see vast inequities between Mexicans that had been naturalized or were born in the United States and those undocumented workers who had crossed the border to work with no money, guarantees, or benefits. When Islas was growing up, he would witness the channeling and control of the Rio Grande's water for energy resale, the mushrooming of foreign-owned factories along the Mexican side of the border, and the strengthening of border surveillance. As globalizing forces of capital increased, the Greater Mexican borderland would become more and more a space that turned the Chicano/Mexicano subjects in El Paso into terrorized, commodified, and exploitable ethnic-object specimens. The contradictory cultural and economic conditions that informed the El Paso/Juárez borderland became an everyday reality for Islas.

As the borderland's tensions and hierarchies grew, so too did the presence in El Paso of upper-class Anglos—and the divide between Mexican Americans and "illegal" Mexican migrants. Islas's own experience of the border revealed much about such hierarchies and divisions within the community. While the new economy allowed a few Mexican Americans (like Islas's mother, who spoke and wrote English) to find jobs (albeit low paying), it ensured that the vast majority would not have access to the educational means for acquiring the skills for decently waged employment. Islas's family was both victim and beneficiary of this system. Jovita's extra income allowed the family to hire unskilled and "illegal" labor from *el otro lado* to help raise the young Arturo and his brothers. Of course, as Islas grew older, he became more aware of his family's participation in this apartheid system of racial and economic separation and hierarchy. As an undergraduate at Stanford he began to formally write his reflections down and invent stories that reflected his experience of a borderland reality. In an expository piece titled "Dear Arturo," written in the late fifties, he says, "The only moments my grandmother became real to me were those times when the well-educated Mexican aristocratic lady would weep because she had to wash the dishes because it was the maid's day off. She taught me to be polite and courteous, which I learned quickly because those qualities endeared me to everyone, except my father" (box 17, folder 1). Islas had become conscious of the hierarchy of difference as an artificial construct that maintained a two-tier society based on a code where whiteness was civilized and darkness was primitive. He was also aware of his parents' exploitation of cheap, imported mestizo labor. He intuited these hierarchies of difference while growing up in El Paso, but was only able to articulate them once he began to set these impressions down on paper. During trips home for holidays, Islas continued to investigate and untangle his family's implicit participation in the racial and social inequities of El Paso. In 1958, for example, he writes how he would "spend as much time in the Mexican [Juárez] bordertown as possible." He continues, "My relatives will not like that. They cannot see why I bother with 'those people'" ("An Existential Document"; box 17, folder 1).

It was partly Islas's growing awareness of the social realities of the border that drew him to literature at Stanford. As an undergraduate, he turned away from a career in science (he entered college intending to be medical doctor) and embraced one that would allow him to write short stories, poems, and critical essays. He saw in writing a way to untangle the racial, sexual, cultural, and political borderland of his childhood and adolescence, a realm that was intensely personal but also political. As an English major he enrolled in many expository and creative writing classes. He also became editor of the undergraduate literary journal, *Sequoia*. Though many of his peers didn't understand his fascination with racial and economic contradictions, many were dazzled by his skill as a writer. Islas worked hard and steadily on his prose, which gained him admission in Hortense Callisher's graduate creative writing seminar when he was a junior. Here he learned to experiment more formally with voice and point of view, finding new expressive possibilities for his fictional detailing of life on the Juárez/El Paso border. In a short story titled "Poor Little Lamb," he invented a third-person narrator to tell the story of Miguel Chávez—a character less concerned with upward mobility than with a need to ground his own body sexually and racially within a mestizo sensibility. Here Islas experimented with how the personal—Miguel's need

to connect with his estranged father, for example—reaches into larger so-
cial contexts: how racism and elitism are internalized by those who are
themselves the victims of racism. Miguel seeks meaning in a present that
is both free of the father and still anchored in his ancestral heritage. In an-
other of Islas's short stories (untitled), he paints in detail the lives of three
border-inhabiting sisters: Clara, Luisa, and Arabella Mendoza. These
mexicana characters are forced to use their gender-inscribed roles as
women within patriarchy to either fall victim to or escape from a violent,
macho world. In this story, Islas chooses to disrupt readerly expectation
by infusing into this U.S./Mexico borderland a strong sense of the me-
tropolis and modernity. Arabella, depicted as very cosmopolitan, smokes
American cigarettes, carries a "glossy black purse," and wears "white-
framed sunglasses" and "orange-colored lipstick" (box 18, folder 1). Islas
is also critical of those characters, like Arabella, who do not use their cos-
mopolitan identity to free themselves, but rather to oppress their fellow
sisters. These women internalize forms of neocolonial oppression rather
than participate in the narrative of liberal white feminism that was ascen-
dant at the time. In the story "Boys with the Eyes of a Fawn," Islas explores
the life of a Juárez prostitute, Theresa. Here Islas uses leitmotif and sym-
bol (veils, vision, and eyes) to critique how patriarchy (both Mexican and
American) uses religion to oppress a racialized and gendered underclass.
And in another short story (untitled), Islas uses the third-person point of
view to fictionalize himself as the character "Art," who crosses to the Mex-
ican side of the El Paso/Juárez border to meet up with his love interest,
J. D. Here, Islas boldly tells the story of love between two young men—
one Chicano, one Anglo—that can surface only when they cross over to
the Mexican side of the border, which Islas mythologizes as a place of free-
dom from both familial surveillance and heterosexism. Tragically, the
young lovers cannot stay in Mexico. After a night of drunken debauchery,
the two wake up in J. D.'s yard, entangled in each other's arms. Art re-
members the scene: "We cried. We sat down on his mother's geraniums
and cried. We stayed there for about two hours until everything started to
clear up and the sky got all pink and the goddamn birds started making a
racket. I told J. D. to go to bed before his mother woke up and saw us. Now,
I wish she had seen us. . . . But J. D. got up and ruined everything by
shaking my hand" (box 18, folder 1).

Fiction would prove to be the means by which Islas could explore personal conflicts and recover experience, and as his interest in writing short stories continued to grow, so did his skill as a storyteller. In his story "Orejas de papalote" ("Dumbo Ears"), Islas transforms autobiography—his child protagonist's ears stick out (as his own did) and he grows up in a patriarchal-ruled, dysfunctional family—into an exploration of childhood generally. Islas delves deeply into his protagonist Faustino García's pain as he is shunned by other children on the playground. After the children mercilessly tease Faustino, he "gasped for air and tried to swallow," with "anger and shame . . . radiating from inside his chest" (box 18, folder 1). Islas probes the relation between this character's anger toward an absent father and his own self-hatred. It turns out that Faustino's pain grows not from being teased for having big ears, but from the fact that he shares this physical trait with his father, who has abandoned him for a white woman. At home, Faustino takes his father's razor blade and cuts himself. In this story, Islas creatively critiques a patriarchal social structure wherein fathers pass on self-hatred from one generation to the next—a self-hatred that translates either into direct acts of physical self-mutilation or into victimization of loved ones.

In other stories written during the 1970s, Islas explores the other end of the spectrum: octogenarians and their experiences within the family. For example, in "Tía Chucha" (which he would later develop into *The Rain God*), he untangles the love and hate that bind together the eponymous character with her grandson, Miguel Chico. Tía Chucha "would have been appalled by the term *Chicano*, but she would have thought César Chávez a saint" (box 12, folder 2) and does not understand her grandson's interest in his Amerindian heritage. She adamantly refuses to acknowledge her own mixed-race identity—she will not wash dishes or clean house, because this is "something for the *criadas* to do." The dark, Amerindian-featured Tía Chucha cannot see that she has internalized this myth of pure Spanish descent, wherein Spanish is pure and civilized and Indian is impure and degenerate—a myth that has been used to justify the exploitation and oppression of mestizo and indigenous populations. In the end, Tía Chucha dies poor and in filth, trapped by her own mythology. Miguel Chico discovers her body, wrapped in dirty sheets, in a house filled with an overwhelming stench, with cats and *cucarachas* everywhere.

In the short stories that Islas wrote during the 1980s, he addressed themes of both racism and queer sexuality. These stories include "The Blind," "Nina," "La familia feliz," "Reason's Mirror," and "Kokkomaa." In "The Blind" (published in San Francisco's prestigious *Zyzzyva* in 1986), Islas invents another grand-matriarchal character, Jesús María. Like Tía Chucha, she believes that she is of a pure Castilian Spanish bloodline; she, too, meets a bitter end when the American and Mexican patriarchal social structure prevents her, as a Mexican American woman, from realizing her dreams. "The Blind" also tells the story of Miguel Chico's love affair with Sam Godwin. The two stories become intertwined when Miguel Chico and Sam travel to Spain, where they agree that "the Jews and the Moors had been responsible for any real culture in a country that Sam said smelled of blood" (box 12, folder 2). Here, the reader is reminded that Jesús María's "pure" Spanish bloodline is the result of colonial violence and of a long history of racial and cultural intermixing (with Jews and Moors, among others) in Spain. In "Reason's Mirror," Miguel Chico learns to control a self-mutilatory impulse that originated from feeling like a sexual outlaw—a queer Chicano shunned by family and society. To take charge of and control his acts of self-destruction, Miguel Chico wrestles with a monster whose carnivorous appetite leaves its breath smelling "of fresh blood and feces" (box 12, folder 2).

NOVEL FORMATIONS

"Día de los muertos"

While Islas wrote many short stories, he was better known as a novelist. The move toward writing longer fictional narratives took place in the mid-1970s. As his sabbatical leave in 1975–76 drew to a close, Islas finished revising the manuscript for his first novel, "Día de los muertos." He wrote this novel as more than an enriching of his creative palette, for he faced the more practical need of publishing a book to present to the English Department's tenure committee.[2] It was somewhat unusual—though not entirely uncommon—for junior faculty to be awarded tenure based on nonacademic manuscripts. "Día de los muertos" was to be such a book. Islas was doubly anxious: "Día" was not only literary; it also dealt with Chicano and queer themes. As he told a reporter, "I knew that such work was not rewarded. The idea in the academy is that critics know more about fiction than those who write it. But there was so little prose fiction written by Mexicans born and educated in this country available for our courses that I chose to write it rather than criticize the little that there was in the late sixties and early seventies" (interview in *Stanford's Grad Minority Recruitment*, 1990; box 1, folder 2). Though he received tenure and moved on to the rank of associate professor, his frustrated attempts to publish this book manuscript—and the others that would follow—continued to be a great source of pain and anxiety. It took him nearly a decade to publish a revised "Día de los muertos" *(The Rain God)* with a small, Palo Alto–based press; and his novel *La Mollie and the King of Tears* only appeared in print seven years after he wrote it and five years after his death.

The world of publishing was a hostile one for Islas. This was not because of a lack of talent on his part, but, as he suspected at the time, because of the novel's experimental content and form. The novel follows the life of a queer Chicano protagonist and shifts between a first- and a third-person narrative point of view. In spite of the great gains in queer civil rights at the time, the publishing world—including the emerging Chicano niche—was still run by homophobic editors. Roger Strauss, of Farrar Strauss, wrote to Islas: "I don't think it is right for us on the basis of this 'taste'" (January 29, 1975; box 5, folder 3). And Macmillan editor Henry William Griffin responded: "Interesting, very interesting indeed, but I'm afraid our sales force would be very hard put to sell a thousand copies" (April 5, 1976; box 5, folder 3). After receiving several such rejection letters early on in his publishing attempts, Islas realized that this would be an uphill battle. He comments in a prefatory note, "It seems to fall neither in the bestseller nor minority literature categories, and publishers, like everyone else, are jealously guarding their pockets. . . . Whatever its fate or the fate of its companion works, *Day of the Dead/Día de los muertos* was written in the spirit of contributing something worthy to Chicano and American letters" (box 7, folder 1). In the mid-1970s, some mainstream publishers were beginning to publish a few Chicano and U.S. Puerto Rican authors. However, these were either of the immigrant farmworker (Galarza) or the urban ghetto (Piri Thomas) variety.[3] Islas's novel did not fit either mold. It was focused on a cast of middle-class Chicano characters and a young man's coming to terms with his queer sexuality. "Día de los muertos" opens with the following: "Uncle Felix was murdered by an eighteen-year-old soldier from the South on a cold, dry day in February" (box 5, folder 4). Mainstream publishers were not ready for what would follow: a complex exploration of queer sexuality within a Chicano family that begins and ends with death. At the time, not only were there few Latino (Chicano, Puerto Rican, Cuban American) writers published, but even fewer authors were published who focused on themes of queer sexuality. (At the time, one of the very few places where one could even find queer-themed literature was the Oscar Wilde bookstore in New York City, where Islas often stopped during his trips east to visit Jay Spears.) In a letter to Islas's New York agent John Meyer, Harper & Row editor Frances McCullough wrote how Islas's exploration of sexual attitudes was "peculiar" and that as a result, the novel was "quite beyond his control" (April 18, 1979; box 7, folder 1), and later John E. Woods at Harcourt Brace wrote to Islas: "There's something strangely bloodless and abstracted about it. I assume in a certain sense Mr. Islas intended this as a device to hold in check some of the rage, craziness, and sexuality of his material" (October 6, 1983; box 7, folder 2).

In spite of the discouraging flow of rejection letters, Islas continued his struggle to publish "Día de los muertos." He found a new literary agent, Bob Cornfield, and revised the novel on the basis of his criticisms. Cornfield said that the novel had "too many stories to tell, too many characters that must be seen," and that it was too "meditative and melodramatic" (letter, May 9, 1978). Islas invented a consistent narrative in the third person, tightened up the plot, and sculpted characterizations anew. In this new version of "Día de los muertos," the characters also spoke less Spanish—and when dialogue did appear in Spanish, Islas made sure that there would be enough context for English-speaking readers to understand. In a letter to friend Anita Smith Paradowski, Islas recalls this process of revision, writing, "Originally, everything Mamá Chona said was written in Spanish and so it was a 'bi-lingual' novel. Ideally, someday, when readers are truly bilingual, it can be published that way. In the meantime, I tried to define the Spanish terms I used as subtly or as ingeniously as possible so as not to jolt the reader out of the atmosphere of the book. I don't know that I succeeded but I had a lot of fun trying" (April 29, 1988). In the same letter, he recalls his decision to create a third-person narrative that would not only smooth out and make consistent the novel's narrative voice but also "avoid making any one of the characters a 'hero' or 'heroine.' The family is the central character. That Chicano life has its own particular way of looking at the concept of family was what I wanted to show." Miguel Chico would become, as Islas tells Paradowski, "the filter through which we see what is going on with these characters in their particular landscape." This third-person narrator also moves back and forward in time, giving the novel a circular feel and, as he himself says much later, "an inner coherence develops and connects scenes" (February 20, 1990; box 53, folder 5). Islas also toned down the protagonist's queer sexuality. With all the sculpting and transformation, "Día de los muertos" was close to the shape it would have when published as *The Rain God*. With Cornfield's blessing, Islas sent out the newly revised "Día" manuscript for another round with the New York publishers.

Mainstream publishers continued to respond to the manuscript negatively during the late 1970s and early 1980s. Many continued to disapprove of its gay content—even in its more gently whispered form—as well as to its focus on a cast of Chicanos who were neither farmworkers nor gangsters. The New York publishing establishment betrayed a parochial vision that, as José David Saldívar astutely says when commenting on Islas's early struggle to publish, "overlooked the complex literary and cross-cultural influences from both North America and Latin America that shape his writing" (1991, 106). Frustrated and angry, Islas decided to be direct in his next cover letter, writing John Dodds at Putnam that "a number of New York houses have turned it down, all with assurance that I am a fine writer and that it is finely done, etc. They simply do not see a market for it. I am very tired of trying to convince them that there *is* an audience for such a work and that it exists west of New Jersey—specifically, the West and Southwest" (undated; box 7, folder 1). The direct plea and rational justification, however, did not help sway

Dodds, who rejected the manuscript. Discouraged with New York publishers, Islas turned his sights to smaller, more local, presses. However, even these kept their doors closed to Islas. After Susan Doran reviewed the manuscript for Fjord press, she wrote Islas that she had been raised "in a predominantly Mexican neighborhood in Los Angeles and [had] close relationships with several large Mexican families, but she did not feel that his characters were Mexican enough"; she concludes that "someone who did not have some knowledge of the characters already would not find enough here to understand them" (February 19, 1983; box 7, folder 1). Islas had had enough of being rejected. Several weeks after receiving Susan Doran's letter, he wrote to her: "I hate it when 'outsiders'—both cultural and literary (in terms of being writers of *fiction*)—talk about my book. . . . You are describing a novel *you* would write from an 'outsider's' point of view. The 'insiders' already know my characters and don't consider them 'flat.' You lack courage and imagination" (March 3, 1983; box 7, folder 1). Islas grew more and more bitter toward what he came to understand as a provincial and homophobic publishing establishment. For Islas, trying to publish a novel like "Día de los muertos" made personal and tangible what he already knew more generally about the manifest destiny outlook of North American colonialism and imperialism: self-replicating Euro-American elites control what is considered culturally tasteful and important for the rest of the country. Islas knew that the editors who deemed the novel tasteless were simply misreading a story that sought to refute stereotypes and bring to life a new set of complexly conceived Chicano/a characters. Islas felt that his novel was perceived as threatening—not because it dealt with racial and sexual mayhem but because it "normalized" but did not mainstream a queer Chicano subjectivity.

By 1982, Islas still had not found a publisher. This became even more disconcerting considering that Chicano/a letters was coming into its own as a complex and contradictory panoply of textual voices. Chicanas such as Cherríe Moraga, Ana Castillo, Sandra Cisneros, and Gloria Anzaldúa were beginning to appear in edited anthologies. And Chicano writer Richard Rodriguez had published his inflammatory *Hunger of Memory*.

Islas became increasingly frustrated as other Chicano/a authors were being published; he also witnessed the rapid ascent of what he considered a group of third-rate Anglo writers who had come out of creative writing workshops. Islas nevertheless continued his struggle, leaning heavily on those around him for support. Many of his colleagues in the English department, he reflected at one point, "thought [the novel] good enough to consider it as part of my tenure qualifications and expressed great optimism that it would be published immediately" (undated note; box 7, folder 2). N. Scott Momaday, Wallace Stegner, and John L'Heureux, as well as literary critics Ian Watt and Albert J. Guerard, thought it worthy of publication (box 7, folder 1). Fellow Chicano writer and colleague at Stanford José Antonio Burciaga wrote that the novel gave the magical realism of Latin American literature "a distinct desert flavor, like mirages," and predicted that it would eventually "stand out in Chicano Literature" (May 27, 1984; box 7, folder 3). And another colleague, Herbert Lindenberger, wrote to Islas that he was "entranced by the whole thing" and that he was very anxious to read a sequel (undated note; box 7, folder 1). Finally, it would be the help of one of Islas's friends and colleagues, Ian Watt, that would prove decisive in getting the manuscript published. Ian Watt introduced Islas to literary agent Ruth Cohen, who worked long and hard to find a publisher and was a great believer in his work. Dismayed with the success of Richard Rodriguez's *Hunger of Memory*, she writes Islas, "Why his book was chosen is clear; why your book is not also published still remains a sad mystery. I KNOW you have a great story" (March 14, 1982; box 31, folder 1). Ruth Cohen finally found a sympathetic editor in Mary Jane Di Piero at Alexandrian Press—a local publisher established by Patrick Suppes, a philosophy professor at Stanford who wanted a venue for his wife to be able to publish her novels. Islas was more than happy. After nearly a decade—and more than thirty-two rejections—"Día de los muertos," revised and retitled as *The Rain God: A Desert Tale*, finally found a home. It was not New York, but the distribution of the book would be large enough for the novel to receive the kind of exposure in and around the San Francisco Bay Area that he knew he could build on for wider recognition.

The Rain God

Soon after *The Rain God* appeared on bookstore shelves in late October 1984, it began to receive local critical and popular acclaim. The first print run of 500 hardbacks sold well enough for Alexandrian Press to print a larger run: 1,500 paperbacks. The paperbacks sold out almost immediately. Word of mouth, along with Islas's ruthless self-promotion, helped ensure continued sales. In a review for the *El Paso Herald-Post,* fellow El Pasoan (and Stanford PhD) Vicki Ruiz celebrates Islas's shaping of fully developed "poignant women characters . . . who live, love and endure," concluding that "whether outspoken or shy, these *mujeres* share an inner strength on which they rely to keep their families together" (1984). And Paul Skenazy, friend and professor at the University of California-Santa Cruz, writes in his review for the *Oakland Tribune* that the novel transforms "family legend into a subtle, quiet fiction that challenges the assumptions we too often bring to ethnic literature [and whose] protest in the novel is more plaintive than outraged" (box 7, folder 5). *The Rain God* is a story, Skenazy continues, "of hyphenated identity . . . where languages and traditions pass uneasily through customs." He also notes that the novel self-reflexively mixes genres, reminding the reader that while the story is informed by reality, it ultimately, as Skenazy comments, "unravels the knotted strands of belief, social experience and cultural myth that become destiny."

Sales figures for *The Rain God* did not match those of Richard Rodriguez's best-selling *Hunger of Memory,* but Chicano/a critics hailed it as a valuable contribution to Chicano literature. For example, Héctor Calderón at Yale thought *The Rain God* should be "read within the politics of literature as a response to *Hunger of Memory.* Richard Rodriguez has played a crucial role in sharpening Islas' distinction between two opposing views of Chicano literature. Islas has been vocal about the pitfalls of yielding to political or elitist interests. The Chicano writer must steer a middle course." Rodriguez, Calderón continues, had argued that the novel "could not give expression to the rich, communal family life and orality of Chicano culture"; Islas's *The Rain God* had proven Rodriguez wrong (review; box 7, folder 5). Calderón's assessment of *The Rain God* as belonging to a Latin American tradition where the private (family) and public (history) intersect was mirrored in other scholarly essays. Erlinda Gonzales-Berry commented on Islas's subtle recuperation of an otherwise over mythologized and/or erased pre-Columbian belief system. According to her interpretation, when the great Nahuatl rain god appears at the death bed of the ultra-Catholic character Mamá Chona, the god invites her to his heaven in a hybrid mixing of pre-Columbian with Judeo-Christian belief (1985, 259). Gonzales-Berry also analyzed the importance of Islas's framing device; his use of a Neruda poem about death to open the novel and his use of the fifteenth-century Aztec rain god poem by Netzahualcóyotl to end the novel, she wrote, reflected the novel's mestizo worldview. By June 1985 *The Rain God* had sold over 3,000 copies. And it continued to sell well enough for a Dutch press to translate and publish the novel as *De Regen god* in 1987. Elated, Islas writes playfully that he could not understand a word, but he liked the "cover immensely" (journal, February 14, 1987; box 55, folder 1).

In the years that followed, the novel would draw a range of Chicano/a responses. Rosaura Sánchez interpreted the novel as a "form of a collective confession, an act of exorcism, a ritual within which the writer is *both* confessor *and* collective sinner" (1991, 119). Marta Sánchez identified Islas's technique of being able to create a "gap between narrator and character and yet having them be one and the same," which leads to, she continued, "the formation of the protagonist's 'I' with no 'I' overtly present at any time" (1990, 286). For her, Islas's invention of a "narrator who calls attention to himself as both subject and object opens up 'new' possibilities for questioning traditional hierarchical relationships within both a Mexican-Chicano culture and a 'dominant' literary tradition. This splitting allows Islas a flexibility toward and an ironic distance from his own limitations and blindness, providing him with a method to analyze his estrangement from himself and his native culture" (287). Roberto Cantú went so far as to identify Mamá Chona as a "human vortex in which two past enemy bloods mingle and flow in continuous pugnacity and self-hatred" (1992, 148). Cantú also notes Islas's use of the number six: six is the number of days it took for the creation of the universe and everything within it, according to the Old Testament, but it was also in the sixth month of the Aztec calendar that nocturnal sacrifices were dedicated to the rain god Tláloc. Cantú argued that Islas's novel redefined the "ethnic self in a postmodern world," thereby rescuing a "collective history from oblivion" (148). Finally, Cantú wrote that Islas, by refiguring the cultural boundaries and histories that delimit individual and collective experience in the United States, "dramatically transcends the thematics of the Chicano cultural movement of the 1960s"; by his "sophisticated handling of narrative emplotment and point of view," he created a novel that was unique in its "critical reexamination of our own cultural discourses" (150). José David Saldívar situated the novel within the Latin American magical realist and Anglo southwestern storytelling genres: "Like the best of Stegner's narratives about the American West, it takes life from the memory of formative events in a specific landscape characterized by migration" (1991, 117). And David Román made visible the narrative's exploration of the "ramifications of a Latino 'gay' subjectivity in cultures that refuse to acknowledge the possibility of such a stance" (1993, 224).[4]

The Rain God was increasingly reviewed, taught, and theorized among Chicano/a scholars, reviewers, and teachers across the country.[5] By 1987, the novel had cycled through eight print runs and sold over 8,000 copies, and, as Islas feared, the Alexandrian Press was simply too small to keep up with the demand, and he started looking for another press. In a letter to editor Toni Burbank at Bantam Books, Islas said he was exploring the possibility of reacquiring his novel's distribution rights and reselling them to another publisher, perhaps Bantam. Burbank wasn't interested. Although the novel's sales in the Bay Area proved that there was a regional demand for it, other publishers showed a clear lack of interest in taking it on. In a letter to Ruth Cohen, senior editor Patricia L. Mulcahy at Penguin, wrote, "I fear that in California THE RAIN GOD would continue to receive fine notices but not sell well enough to be worth taking on" (October 21, 1985; box 7, folder 1). Similarly, Avon Books senior editor John Douglas commented, "Although it is nicely written I simply don't see this as a book that is likely to find a significant audience in mass market paperback form. It would be a hard book to categorize in an industry that deals more and more in categories. It is also, despite the good writing, a book that I read more as an obligation than as a pleasure" (December 23, 1985; box 7, folder 1).

In pursuit of his publishing goals, Islas became a ruthless self-promoter. Toughened by years of rejection letters—but heartened by respectable sales numbers and critical appreciation—Islas took every opportunity he could to promote his work: bookstore readings, creative writing conferences, and at his English literature lectures at Stanford. No opportunity was missed; he even promoted himself in a letter to the Whitting Award committee, nominating one of his own creative writing students: "At the risk of being immodest, may I suggest my own work for your consideration? Though my publication record is modest, it has achieved critical notice and some distinction" (box 40, folder 16). He concludes, "I feel at a very critical stage of my career. Further recognition, especially from your program, and encouragement are more than welcome." Needless to say, the committee did not consider self-nominations.

Islas also wanted out of his contract with Ruth Cohen, hoping to find a better known agent. Islas finally found his agent, the well-known Sandra Dijkstra, who soon signed with a New York publisher. Avon, which had rejected the book in 1985, bought the paperback rights in 1990, and *The Rain God* swiftly became one of the best selling and most widely acclaimed novels in Chicano/a letters.

The Rain God is a novel informed by many personal experiences—Islas's growing up within a culturally vibrant and hybrid U.S./Mexico borderland filled with contradiction—and by many different world literary storytelling traditions. The writing of *The Rain God* was a way for Islas to connect and understand the contradictions and paradoxes of home: the cold and hot memories of his childhood in a desert borderland that destroyed and made for new, stronger forms of life. The El Paso/Juárez borderland was a geographical and cultural space that, as he writes, provided a "spiritual metaphor for my work, which includes mostly desert people. I like thinking that the desert—in all its glorious light—was once the bottom of the sea. Writing is like going into the desert by yourself" (journal, September 25, 1988; box 29, folder 3). In *The Rain God* Islas sought to capture such a complexly layered and paradoxical desert borderland, noting in 1990 how it is such a "landscape and its peoples [that] I write about in

my fictions. And like some of my characters, I have led a double life be-
tween cultures, between languages, between sexes, between nations, be-
tween two compelling and different ways of looking at the world" ("Cul-
tural Identity and the Crisis of Representation"; box 29, folder 9). Islas
struggled for many years to find the voice to be able to express such a bor-
derland space, finally discovering Southern gothic narrative realism and
Latin American magical realism as appropriate storytelling modes that
would give shape to what he called his "collection of tragi-comic tales"
("Selling Myself by Arturo Islas"; box 7, folder 2). Islas carved out a new
storytelling voice as he hybridized the many genres and styles found in
literature on both sides of the U.S./Mexico border and beyond. He used
this voice to chart the many symbolic and real borderlands (cultural, lin-
guistic, racial, and sexual) that threatened to destroy but also to create new
forms of life: Chicanos/as struggling to inhabit a threatening and life-
giving borderland world.[6]

Islas not only drew from literary influences north and south of the bor-
der, but also looked to the east and beyond. At one point, he imagined
himself as a writer working alongside not just writers from Latin Amer-
ica and the United States, but also writers from England, Russia, France,
and Spain—all writing "novels at once in a circular room" ("Cultural
Identity"). Thus he did not imagine himself as a writer confined by a sin-
gle direction of influence and circumscribed by national literary canons:
he actively studied the craft of Cervantes's picaresque, Flaubert's search
for *bon mot* stylistics and perfect syntax, Proust's narrative phrasing and
temporality, García Márquez's magical realism, Forster's queer aesthetic,
Stendhal's realism, Faulkner's Southern gothic, Conrad's impressionistic
technique, and Turgenev's patrilineal epic form. Islas especially admired
and emulated Henry James's later work; he felt that James captured, as he
remarked on one occasion, "not so much what people say to one another,
but the atmosphere they create between them when they say it" (box 23,
folder 3). He also emulated Hemingway's dexterous use of syntax and
diction to express the nuance of emotion. (Hemingway was a writer he
had long admired, often recalling with fondness his first encounter with
The Old Man and the Sea in his high school library.) Nabokov, whose *Lolita*
he much admired, was the supreme stylistic genius for Islas—achieving

what he once called an "aesthetic paradise"—and one of the writers he pays homage to in *The Rain God*, naming one of his characters Lola. He was also drawn to James Baldwin, who had a deep impact on him. Both men were marginalized by their respective ethnic communities because of their gay sexual identification; Islas also had great respect for Baldwin's skill and success at "portraying gay male characters in a non-stereotypical way" (1990a, 29). Like Baldwin, Islas was "tired of the claptrap both in and out of fiction that's written about gay people, gay males in particular." And like Baldwin, Islas conceived of himself as an "ethnic" American writer, but one who wanted to complicate the Chicano/a experience; he found a kindred spirit in Baldwin, who struggled against nationalist currents that essentialized racial identity.[7]

In the same disciplined spirit with which he studied the craft of other writers, Islas worked on his own writing, for he was a perfectionist when it came to his craft.[8] For Islas, "all writing is rewriting," as he often commented. And, like another of Islas's revered writers, Flaubert, he believed in finding the precise word to express character and emotion and to paint the appropriate descriptive landscape. Each of Islas's novels went through at least five radical transformations. After first typing the manuscript, he would use pen and pencil to write, erase, and rewrite; then he would type it over again. Once Islas discovered that he had a talent as a writer, he dedicated much time and energy to carving prose and story lines. Islas worked long and hard, but he often enjoyed the work, feeling himself fortunate when he could sit in front of that "scary blank page" and fill it up with "a wonderful combination of thoughts and feelings" ("Freshman Class" speech; box 30, folder 24). As far as Islas was concerned, everyone had access to the raw material needed to become a writer. However, as he told his students, "most of us in this life will be too lazy [or are] too distracted to draw from that obscurity within ourselves that which is truly ours and offer it (not necessarily in writing) to the world" (Hemingway lecture; box 23, folder 12). He was also a writer who liked routine—writing late at night or early in the morning on the same typewriter, his Smith Corona—until it began to break down and he had to buy a JUKI 2200, "with all sorts of gadgets." Islas modified his writing process in the late 1980s, with the PC revolution, buying an IBM. He would no longer mark up and cut out (often with scissors) to reshape manuscripts, but used the computer to erase and cut/paste. Also, Islas was a writer who felt that a novel was never quite finished.

For Islas, "one is a writer when one is writing" ("Freshman Class" speech; box 30, folder 24) and when one is wide awake to the complexities, smells, flavors, sights, and sounds of life. Fiction for Islas was the transforming of such "real" smells, flavors, sights, and sounds into the expansive possibilities of the imagination that narrative fiction offered. He once commented, "If you are a writer, you are constantly preoccupied not only with your own relationship to those others who are not you, but also with their relationship to each other, quite apart from you. That's where a writer's imagination comes in" (Hemingway lecture; box 23, folder 12). The process was central and critical to his life. His many brushes with death made him acutely aware of everyday experience—especially with an eye to transforming the "sordid, happy/unhappy facts of life into art" (letter to Nick Brommell, June 1983; box 42, folder 11)— but also it was in the process of writing that the fictions themselves would help sustain him in the face of his own life's tragic turns. His fiction and the fictional worlds created by others opened the doors to that special place where he could experience vicariously a body, emotions, and thoughts different from his own. He believed that adventures were not only to be had in the "real" world, but also in those experiences that "occur within" and that "are inward not outward" (Hemingway lecture). A writer like Emily Dickinson, he wrote, "knew this in her bones and remained in the privacy of her room and garden" (Hemingway lecture). For Islas, "true and serious writers . . . know that there is more to writing than simply describing adventures or events. Experience means attributing meaning to our adventures, or to put it another way, it means giving shape and form to chaos" (Hemingway lecture).

Writing and reading for Islas was all about how one could transform oneself and others through such vicarious experience. To succeed as a writer, he felt he had to reshape personal experience into something that would echo beyond the self. He writes of such a process: "What I think a talented writer does *in part* is to create characters out of different fragments of his/her personality. And with the necessary help of the imagination, of reason, of inspiration, he/she can transform them into what appear to the reader to be separate and real people when, in fact, they are exaggerations of accurate portrayals of the monstrous and angelic fragments which exist within him or herself" (Hemingway lecture).[9] Islas's view of what counted as good literature was founded on how well a writer could transform personal experience. Islas saw Fitzgerald as a writer who managed to invent novels removed from the author's direct experience and yet who managed to create and give order to a "a self or *persona* who has lived through events they did not have when experiencing them" (Hemingway lecture). For Islas, such writers *"always* modify the effects of the evidence, and sometimes transform it entirely" (Hemingway lecture). Writing narrative fictions, Islas says, is all about how the writer adjusts and reconciles "the human element with a bundle of various things not human" (Four great novels lecture; box 23, folder 9). To summarize, Islas believed that novel writing involves reshaping storytelling voices and genres and laboring hard to transform personal experience—direct or gained vicariously by reading other fictions—into something with meaning beyond the private self.

La Mollie and the King of Tears

Six months after *The Rain God* received the Border Regional Library Association Award in 1986, Islas set out to write his second novel, *La Mollie and the King of Tears*—a narrative fiction that moved him away from his more autobiographically oriented first novel. When Islas first sat down to write *La Mollie*, he imagined it not as a sequel to *The Rain God* but as a stand-alone "picaresque novel" (his words) set in San Francisco. Islas had always been interested in the Iberian-peninsular picaresque tradition and its various transnational manifestations. As early as 1962, Islas wrote a graduate seminar paper comparing the translation and transformation of the *pícaro* figure as he crossed from Spain to Britain, studying at length writers Lazarillo de Tormes and Thomas Nashe. Something about the *pícaro* intrigued Islas. He was a figure who inhabited the social and racial margins. The *pícaro* moved at the edges of different social landscapes and could see (and make visible to the reader) the very diverse

strata and underbelly of society in its everyday operations. Islas identi-
fied strongly with this figure and wanted at some point to invent a *pícaro*
character. So, when Islas began a year of teaching at the University of
Texas-El Paso in the fall of 1986, he told his class of creative writing stu-
dents to imagine someone completely different from them and to speak
in that character's voice alone. This was as much an exercise for Islas as
it was for the students. Inspired by José Montoya's poem "El Louie," Islas
invented the Tejano-born and raised pachuco *pícaro* Louie Mendoza,
whose Spanglish street-slang *(caló)* poetic expressed a worldview radi-
cally different from Islas's earlier, more autobiographically informed
Miguel Chico of *The Rain God*. Islas first called Louie Mendoza's story
"The Lame"; it would later be completed and published (posthumously)
as *La Mollie and the King of Tears*.

While his students were working on their assignment in the fall of
1986, Islas holed up in his parents' study (he lived with his parents on
Mesita Street during this 1986–87 academic year) and, as if possessed,
churned out page after page of "The Lame." In early November Islas had
sixty polished pages and by the first week of January 1987 he was already
nearing the end of the novel: "14–15 pp. of a first draft of Part IV of 'The
Lame' done" (journal, January 8, 1987; box 55, folder 1). One week later,
after teaching his last class for the day, he drove to his parents' house,
downed a cup of coffee, sat down in his study, and wrote the conclusion.
Afterward, he writes in his journal, "I think it's going to be a lay down
slam? Where is it coming from? I don't know" (journal, January 14, 1987).
Once the first draft of the manuscript was finished, Islas took a rest, re-
turning to revise the book in the spring. On June 25, Islas completed the
final revisions. He writes in his journal, "I can feel that I'm tiring of him
and my imagination is aching for something else. That's good!" (June 25,
1987; box 55, folder 1).

As Islas gave flesh to Louie Mendoza's physical vigor and charismatic
street presence, a character emerged completely opposite to *The Rain
God*'s more subdued, physically troubled, and book-smart Miguel Chico.
Stylistically, too, Islas proved he could radically shift gears—from the
mythopoetic mode of *The Rain God* to a gritty realism. As I have said else-
where, in *La Mollie* "there's a mystery to solve, and Islas's Louie uses

short, quick Dashiell Hammett-style sentences to unfurl it" (2000, 583). Also, as I have pointed out before, Islas gives new form to the *roman* noir genre when he employs a storytelling frame that "shifts from the white, hetero-masculine subject *à la* Chandler to the *pachuco, caló* speaking and troping Louie Mendoza" (583).

Even though "The Lame" is less autobiographical, it still contains biographical fact, which tends to soften the story's otherwise hard, macho edges, investing the narrative with a positive queer sensibility. Louie's brother is identified as gay—and a frequenter of S&M clubs (like Islas in the 1970s); and Louie's best friend, Virgil Spears (a play on Jay Spears, Islas's ex-partner), is also gay. The name Virgil Spears not only alludes to Dante's guide, but also combines Jay's last name and the first name from a story that Arturo Sr. told Islas ("Sonny") when he came out to the family: "Sonny, the first man who beat me up was a homosexual. I'll never forget him. He was more macho than anything and I still remember his name—Virgil Randall" (transcribed phone conversation, February 20, 1977; box 53, folder 4). At one point, Islas explicitly refashions fact, writing in his journal: "Work on ending to "The Lame"; it's there w/ some surprises. I get to use J's line: "And yet I wish but for the thing I have" (journal, January 15, 1988).

As the fictional Louie took on a life of his own, he proved more and more to be a composite of the many shards of Islas's life. When Islas worked as an educational therapist at the Menlo Park V.A. hospital in the sixties, he met an ex-pachuco, Mr. Martínez, who would, Islas writes, become "transformed through fiction into Louie Mendoza" (Stanford class of 1990 speech; box 30, folder 19). "The Lame" was thus inspired by José Montoya's fictional "El Louie," Mr. Martínez, Islas's younger brother Louie, and his father. As Islas notes, Louie speaks "in a dialect I know well because my father speaks it" (California Teachers Association lecture, February 1988; box 29, folder 2). Islas also recreated his El Paso High School experience, fictionalizing his own English and Latin teachers as the composite character Leila P. Harper, who has a big influence on Louie Mendoza's life. Islas concludes of "The Lame": "In retrospective fashion, Louie is telling us about his life and education in a public school Texas border town while he is waiting in the San Francisco Hospital emergency room to find out what has happened to La Mollie. She has fallen and injured the back of her head quite badly" (class of 1990 speech). Louie Mendoza, however, does more than tell his story.[10] By telling his story, he

> provides the fluid container for him to re-experience the many spatialized selves that co-exist palimpsestically and come to inform the Louie-as-narrating-subject. Louie doesn't experience the sort of epiphany that traditionally identifies a character's dialectical synthesis of the encountered other, but rather he comes to co-exist as a straight, thirtysomething *pachuco* with a vision that queers binary oppositioned world-city spaces. For queer author Arturo Islas, then, straight Louie's *queer* re-territorializing of traditionally white, hetero-controlled ethnosexualized ex-centric spaces builds a politics of resistance that expands beyond sexual-object choice (male-male, female-female, female-male) to make room for a straight-inclusive queerspace imaginary. (Aldama 2000, 591)

While Islas wrote "The Lame" as if possessed, he was not sure how the publishing world would take to it. At one point, just before revising the manuscript to send it to his editor, Maria Guarnaschelli at William Morrow (at this point, Islas was negotiating a contract for the sequel to *The Rain God*), he writes in his journal, "Continuing thoughts that no one but me will care about L. Mendoza" (January 13, 1987). As a backup, Islas sent a letter to his new agent, Sandra Dijkstra, writing, "Let me introduce you to my Chicano Huckleberry Finn, Louie Mendoza. He's older than Huck (about a century), knows women (I'm not sure the verb is correct there) and has captured my imagination for almost an entire year" (June 29, 1987; box 7, folder 10). Islas kept his fingers crossed, anxious about whether Sandra Dijkstra and Maria Guarnaschelli would like it. If they did not, he knew that he would have to "fight hard for it," as he wrote in his journal on January 30, 1987.

Learning from past experience with publishers, Islas decided not to wait for Sandra Dijkstra and Maria Guarnaschelli to respond before sending "The Lame" to others for comment and review. First, Islas spoke with friend and colleague Paul Skenazy, at the University of California-Santa Cruz, about the manuscript; Skenazy made some suggestions and Islas immediately began reworking it. By the time agent Sandra Dijkstra phoned him back with her response—"she loves Louie Mendoza. She mentions something about getting my 'gay' things in it and wants me to call it La Mollie" (journal, August 3, 1987; box 55, folder 1)—Islas had already crafted a new version of the novel. The retitled "Chakespeare in the Barrios or The King of Tears" (box 15, folder 1) would garner praise from colleague Diane Middlebrook, who writes him how she "read this in 2 big gulps—couldn't put it down. I really enjoyed it, all the way through" (September 11, 1987). Middlebrook's enthusiastic response to the narrative, with its texturing of such "various and zesty worlds," and her praise of Louie's deft characterization of "his neurotic defensiveness and his genuisness" greatly encouraged Islas. Middlebrook's laudatory comments were not made without some critical feedback, however. She recommended, for example, that he more fully flesh out the woman love interest La Mollie and discard any material—the epigraphs, notes, and the seemingly artificial presence of an academic critic character—so that the novel would *show* more than didactically *tell* Louie's story. She concludes her letter, "Louis is fresh and interesting enough to carry the novel without the burden of literary allusion on the one hand or the quite reductive and I think clumsy device of scholarly notes worked up by a pretentious asshole, on the other. I think the apparatus would drive the readers away, not draw them in—as I was drawn, at once, by Louie's voice" (September 11, 1987). Encouraged by Middlebrook's love of Louie and suggestions for amplifying the reader's engagement of his world, Islas revised the manuscript accordingly.

While agent Sandra Dijkstra—as well as close colleagues Diane Middlebrook and Paul Skenazy—was taken with Louie Mendoza, others rejected him. William Morrow editor Maria Guarnaschelli wrote to Islas: "The book, for me, is not a novel but a harangue. . . . the voice is too inconsistent to hold the reader—it is an incongruous mixture of streetwise and sophisticated" (September 18, 1987; box 7, folder 9). Islas replied angrily that he refused to provide "sugary portraits" of Chicanos and that New York publishing houses were "not ready for an American Hispanic voice that does not do that dance for readers who want to be entertained by 'local color'" (December 2, 1987; box 7, folder 9). In many ways, Islas's angry response to Guarnaschelli was really directed at New York publishers in general; it was also a response that grew from his frustration as a writer who knew he had very little time left. He was aware at this point that he was HIV positive. Given a little time to cool off, Islas returned to the manuscript with Guarnaschelli's comments in mind, tightening up the plot and making the narrative voice more consistent. Harper and Row editor Craig Nelson rejected *La Mollie,* writing, "I'm sorry to have to report that I wasn't taken with the narrator's voice in LA MOLLIE; it just wasn't on the same level of distinction as the stories and the other characters in this book" (February 22, 1988; box 7, folder 10). And in spite of his angry reply to Guarnaschelli, Islas sent a new version to her, at her request. She again rejected the manuscript. Islas then sent it to the University of New Mexico Press, which he thought might be more Chicano friendly. However, he would again meet with rejection. Editor Elizabeth C. Hadas wrote him a letter telling him the press was not prepared to take the "plunge with this novel. Rest assured that I did not send the manuscript out of the house. I read part of it and then gave it to our editorial intern, a young Mexican American woman with a special interest in Chicano literature. We don't feel that it's right for us. Probably if we ever do publish an original novel it will have a New Mexico setting" (October 30, 1990; box 8, folder 1). Islas's efforts failed. He never saw *La Mollie and the King of Tears* published. In an ironic twist of fate, it would be that very press, originally too nervous "to take the plunge," that would publish the novel posthumously in 1996.

Migrant Souls

The period when Islas wrote *La Mollie and the King of Tears* in the late 1980s was filled with unsteady emotion. He would feel ecstatic about coming into his own as a writer—buoyed by *The Rain God*'s popularity and the ease with which he wrote *La Mollie and the King of Tears*—only to slip into deep depression. More and more frequently, anxiety and self-doubt about writing would seize Islas: not only did he receive letters from publishers rejecting *La Mollie and the King of Tears* but also he got a spate of negative responses to a sample chapter ("A Perfectly Happy Family") from his sequel to *The Rain God.* Editors from Penguin, Faber and Faber, William Heinemann, Harcourt Brace, and HarperCollins all replied with letters that chimed an all-too-familiar tune: "It's good but too Latin and very foreign," as HarperCollins's editor Carol O'Brien wrote (box 7, folder 10).

In spite of these setbacks, Islas persevered. With Sandra Dijkstra's New York connections and her unfaltering faith in his creative vision, Islas was finally able to attract the attention of William Morrow. Impressed both by a chapter of the new novel published later as a short story titled "The Blind," in *Zyzzyva* (in 1988), and by *The Rain God*, William Morrow editor Maria Guarnaschelli asked Islas if he would come on board as one of her writers. On January 6, 1987, Islas received his advance contract from Guarnaschelli and called Sandra Dijkstra to share the good news. He could not believe it: Morrow "wanted a 75,000–100,000 word book by July 15 of this year" (journal, January 6, 1987; box 2, folder 1). Islas finally realized his dream: at long last, his work would be published by a New York house and reach a national readership.

With an advance contract in hand, and invigorated after finishing a first draft of *La Mollie and the King of Tears*, in January 1987 Islas began writing what would become *Migrant Souls* (now mystifyingly out of print). He decided that he would again use the narrative technique of fictionalizing autobiographical fact to revisit the U.S./Mexico border town setting of his first novel, Del Sapo (in Spanish this anagram of El Paso translates playfully as "from the toad"), during the 1950s and early 1960s. The setting and characters would be the same as in *The Rain God*, including Miguel Chico, but this time around he wanted to focus on the women in the Angel family—especially the young generation of women, who were willing to act and speak against the family's restrictive sexist and racist codes of conduct. Here Islas shifted from the use of a third-person point of view resting somewhere near Miguel Chico's shoulder in *The Rain God* to a third-person point of view resting somewhere near characters like Josie Salazar, Miguel's divorced cousin. Miguel Chico still appears, but more as a secondary figure who can relate to the other outcast characters from the sidelines. As in *The Rain God*, Islas invented characters who blurred the border between biographical fact and narrative fiction—but here Islas also blurred the borders between his novels. For example, in *Migrant Souls* he included intertextual tie-ins not just to *The*

Rain God but also to *La Mollie.* Thus, at one point Harold (Josie's wife) meets a blonde woman whose name, Harold relates, is "Mollie something or other. She's from a well-known San Francisco family, and she was talking to me about all these groups starting up in the area where people take off their clothes and raise their consciousness" (1991, 187). And the *curandero* Manitas de Oro is first described lighting incense that "Louie Mendoza had sent him from San Francisco during the hippie era" (139). Islas also drew from a variety of other literary sources—especially those he thought were written in the spirit of autobiographical fiction. He alluded directly to Colette's same-sex erotic fictionalized autobiography *Pure and the Impure* in naming one of his characters "Colette" and investing her with French author Colette's love for her "fat and gorgeous silver blue cat" (19). Also, Islas named the lesbian schoolteacher character "Marguerite," again directly alluding to *Pure and the Impure,* where the lesbian Marguerite Moreno is the protagonist and narrator's Spanish lover. While Islas was writing *Migrant Souls,* he read and reread many autobiographical novels and poems. For instance, he studied carefully F. Scott Fitzgerald's *This Side of Paradise*—a novel that, he scribbled in his journal, gave him "ideas for the Miguel Chico section" (January 20, 1987). And when Islas finished a draft of the chapter "The Deaf," he wrote in his journal, "Aren't my little Indians beautiful" (July 25, 1987), alluding to the deep impact William Carlos Williams's poetic lines— "Why don't these Indians get over this nauseating prattle about their souls and their loves and sing us something else for a change"—had on Islas. He also alluded to old-guard Chicano writers like Luis Leal (who praised an early draft of *Migrant Souls)* and Rolando Hinojosa. Thus, Islas invented the character Sancho, who visits "Don Luis Leal's Famous Tex-Mex Diner"; and he named his Korean War veteran character "Tano Hinojosa," who, like the biographical author Rolando Hinojosa, nearly lost a leg in that war.

In January 1987, Islas worked on *Migrant Souls* in the study at his parents' house on Mesita Drive. The place had seemed to release an unstoppable flow when he was writing the first draft of *La Mollie and the King of Tears,* so he thought he would try his luck there again. He launched into the first chapter—"The Deaf"—with great vigor. He took breaks only to sleep, eat, teach at the University of Texas-El Paso—and reconceive plot lines and passages already written. The rhythm worked well, and within a month he had already written the bulk of "The Deaf." Once Islas had a draft of a chapter, he would set out to sculpt and shape it. Of such a process in the writing of "The Deaf," he writes in his journal, "I've got to pare down, write scenes instead of historical narrative" (February 1, 1987; box 2, folder 1). As the months passed, Islas found that his parents' study was, again, a space in which be could imagine and write fruitfully. *Migrant Souls* became his obsession. Even when he took time off from writing because of family obligations or teaching duties, he never stopped revising in his mind characters, plots, and scenes. He writes in his journal, "I'm trusting that my characters—Josie and Miguel Chico— are growing without my guidance in this hiatus" (April 21, 1987; box 2, folder 1).

Migrant Souls continued to grow at a rapid pace—and necessarily so, as his deadline for William Morrow was fast approaching. After Islas finished teaching the spring semester at UTEP, he returned to his home in Palo Alto to continue writing *Migrant Souls*. Far from his parents' study, the pen continued to flow. He writes in his journal, "I don't know where it's coming from, but I don't care" (July 10, 1987; box 2, folder 1). With the chapters on Josie finished, Islas began to develop the priest character, Gabriel (inspired by Islas's ex-priest brother Mario). He also decided to take readers across the border into a Mexican border town. Though Islas missed William Morrow's July deadline for the manuscript, he was confident that he would be able to send Maria Guarnaschelli the manuscript sometime in the fall of 1987. However, once Islas returned to teaching a full load of classes in addition to department duties back at Stanford, he found it difficult to find the time to write. He put on hold social commitments and scraped together those few late-night and early-morning hours to work on his narrative. Not surprisingly, this phase of his writing was not as fluid as that in El Paso, with Islas often writing in his journal of the difficulty of sustaining a narrative plotline because of the fragmented hours in which he wrote. The writing was often "slow," "tortuous," like "typing under water, not as much physically as psychologically. Horrible" (November 2, 1987; box 2, folder 1). During this period, far from family and the peace and quiet of the desert, Islas also struggled to keep at bay destructive alcohol and drug habits he had come to associate with his San Francisco Bay Area lifestyle. To keep clean and maintain the necessary stamina for writing, Islas continued with his treatment in AA and spent time meditating at home, occasionally going to health-spa retreats. The new daily habits—as opposed to the old ones of drinking alcohol and snorting lines of cocaine—helped Islas maintain a sustained and regular creative progression. Often, too, the writing process would help Islas overcome other self-destructive behavioral patterns: a suppressed anger that would boil up occasionally and a pervasive feeling of self-doubt. The writing also provided a venue for Islas to vent some of the frustration and anger he felt when, on January 14, 1988, he was diagnosed HIV-positive. Writing, rewriting, and then finely sculpting *Migrant Souls* into a novel took longer than Islas had expected and his editor wanted, but it served as a pressure release valve, a constant reminder of his vitality, and a way to escape and overcome feelings of being diseased and being a sexual pariah. Writing was a way for him to appease his demons, which would, he writes in his journal, "eat my brains w/out mercy" (August 16, 1988). Finally, as much as the writing of *Migrant Souls* fed his demons and made him feel alive, more than anything else, it became a reason to fight the disease to stay alive: "God, keep me healthy and alive enough to complete this!" he writes in his journal on May 11, 1988.

In September 1988 (thirteen months after William Morrow had fixed the deadline), Islas finally sent his completed manuscript of *Migrant Souls* to agent Sandra Dijkstra and editor Maria Guarnaschelli. Dijkstra's reaction to the novel was mixed, which sent Islas into a minor depression: "It's clear that she completely misread the ending. She was tired when she read it and has sent it back to Laurie to read. I'm stunned by her insensitivity and carelessness. I tell her about Maria's positive reactions. She tells me about Amy Tan's good fortune—again. I'm getting real tired of this!" (October 22, 1988; box 55, folder 2). What with Dijkstra's response, along with his struggle with HIV-related pneumonia, he nearly gave up on the book. It didn't help that his friends Ruth and Ian Watt, whom Islas normally turned to for support during difficult emotional times, also disliked the novel, telling him that it was too maudlin in spirit and that the narrator told the reader too much. Islas felt betrayed and developed a strong bitterness toward the Watts. However, editor Maria Guarnaschelli stood by Islas and continued to show a "passionate devotion" to the novel. She asked for certain revisions but remained committed to its publication. Islas went back to the manuscript he thought he had finished, and continued to rework and revise it through the fall of 1988. In 1989, Islas was free of the manuscript as it went into production with an expected publication date of early 1990.

On January 11, 1990, Islas received his first copy of *Migrant Souls* from William Morrow. His hard work had paid off. By the end of the month, 6,000 copies of *Migrant Souls* had hit Bay Area bookstore shelves. The novel sold out within a month, taking it to the top of *San Francisco Chronicle*'s top-ten best-seller list. That famous writers such as Denise Levertov and Adrienne Rich had given the novel their seal of approval—blurbing the dust jacket—also helped win it critical praise. And the novel was to be reviewed in the *New York Times* book review section. Islas writes in his journal: "I can hardly believe my ears" (January 11, 1990; box 55, folder 4). Islas felt that he had finally realized his goal: to be read not only as a Chicano writer, but as an author recognized nationally—a writer contributing more widely and deeply to the American literary landscape. With *Migrant Souls'* overnight success, sales of *The Rain God* went up, too, sending it into its twelfth and final printing with Alexandrian Press; it would find a new home with Avon.

After a month of publishing fanfare, *Migrant Souls* garnered, at best, mixed reviews in the mainstream press. In the *San Francisco Chronicle*, Henry Mayer wrote that while "it misses the striking originality of the earlier book [Islas still commands the] ability to collapse time and convey intractable conflict in a few telling strokes" (1990, 3). And David Rieff (critic Susan Sontag's son) concluded a review for the *Los Angeles Times* with this snappy bite: "Islas is as wooden a writer as he is acute an observer. . . . We need a great realistic novel about the border. Had Islas written less self-indulgently, that book might have been 'Migrant Souls'" (1990, 3). Islas was disturbed by Rieff's review and thought that he had misread his narrative technique, which collapsed time/space to re-vision the self-as-collective in nonlinear historical time. The *New York Times* review said that Islas held the reader at arm's length and that the characters' "suffering fails to move us" (Unger 1990, 30). In early March, Islas opened the book review section to the *Nation,* hoping that Jeff Gillenkirk's review would be a more thorough and sensitive reading of *Migrant Souls.* Islas was pleased with Gillenkirk's sympathetic comment that the novel was nuanced, but he was not too happy with Gillenkirk's conclusion that the novel was a "sprawling, sociobiological organism with a genealogical tree as convoluted as the L.A. freeway system" and that Islas's attempt "to cross the gender border . . . leaves most of his *Migrant Souls* wandering in the desert" (1990, 314). Generally, he felt that the mainstream reviewers did not understand fully Latin American magical realism, and that some of them were more interested in promoting their own writing at the expense of providing a fair evaluation of his novel.

Much to Islas's delight, the sales figures continued to soar and reviews by the nonmainstream press continued to lavish critical acclaim on *Migrant Souls.* Renato Rosaldo, Marta Sánchez, and Teresa McKenna, to name a few, were enthusiastic about *Migrant Souls'* style and content. In a review for the *El Paso Times,* Mimi Gladstein writes, for example, "Islas is an insightful writer: his characters ring with the authenticity born of a keen insight into the working of the human heart in conflict with itself. *Migrant Souls* is a compelling novel written in a way that both instructs and moves the reader" (1990, 2D). Soon after the novel's publication, many Chicano/a critics began to write scholarly essays on the author and his work. In one of them, "Historical Imagination in Arturo Islas," Antonio C. Márquez identifies the shift from Islas's thematizing of Amerindian belief in *The Rain God* to a clash between a modern secular and a Catholic worldview as they entangle at sites of internalized oppression in *Migrant Souls.* Teresa McKenna not only dedicated her book, *Migrant Song,* to Islas but also used the novel's insistent shift from calling Chicanos "immigrants" to calling them "migrants" as the basis for her articulation of a Chicano/a literary analysis and epistemology. McKenna concludes of Islas's work that its "deep and humanistic" themes work to move Chicano literature "into the twentieth century" (1997, 20). Roberto Cantú analyzes literary techniques in *Migrant Souls* to convey Islas's

postcolonial critique of "Mexicans/Anglo-Americans as *absolute* oppo-
sites (one as 'conquered,' the other as conqueror, racist, etc.), [focusing]
instead on how language itself becomes the framework which both de-
limits and defines our daily conflicts, thereby making it possible to ques-
tion the 'natural' order of the cultural world" (1992, 151). Cantú con-
cludes that "Islas advances other narrative dimensions to a higher
aesthetic level, returning with a stronger force to a form of cultural criti-
cism that touches on discursive practices that determine the way readers
interpret their immediate social world" (153). And Renato Rosaldo's "Fa-
bles of the Fallen Guy" identifies the novel's powerful critique of inter-
nalized colonialism within the Chicano/a community. For those familiar
with Chicano/a letters, Islas's *Migrant Souls* had broken new ground: it
was hailed as one of the most powerful Chicano/a novels to radically
contest those pure (Spanish) and impure (mestizo) colonialist ideologies
that many within the Chicano/a community internalize and continue to
perpetuate. Rosemary Weatherston demonstrates how the novel destabi-
lizes "naturalized" narratives of racial purity and national belonging to
fully explore the conflictive role of the ethnic writer, seeing Islas as a
writer who both serves as the voice of a community and seeks to sidestep
readings of his novel as only ethnography (see Aldama 2005).

POETIC PERFORMANCES

Islas's short stories and novels fictionalize biographical fact and compli-
cate characterizations of old and young Chicanos/as inhabiting cultural,
linguistic, national, and ideological borderland spaces. Islas used a vari-
ety of narrative techniques to achieve this effect, including the unravel-
ing of narrative voice—especially in *The Rain God* and *Migrant Souls*—
often using the densely compact style of poetry to open readers' eyes to
an expansively imagined story world. Saldívar astutely identifies how in
such a narrative technique "moral attitude is defined not only by the log-
ical content of the work, but by the writer's emotional reaction to its
ideas" (1991, 115). As Saldívar notes, Islas's mythopoetic novels have an
Yvor Wintersian poetic sensibility. Indeed, before Islas began writing

novels, he wrote poetry. In 1960, Islas took a course titled "Chief American Poets" with Winters. This was the beginning of what would become an insatiable appetite to learn how to craft poetic verse. So, alongside his more theoretical studies as a PhD student in English, Islas began to train as a poet under Winters's aegis, formally studying and mastering the use of enjambment, apostrophe, synesthesia, and the lyrical iamb, for example.

Under Winters's strong and steady guidance, Islas came into a poetic sensibility wherein he learned to use a suggestive and richly imagined poetic language to transform personal experience into something beyond itself.[11] He learned, according to the Wintersian "poetics of rationality," to balance vivid and emotional poetic language with a more cerebrally driven symbolism. He learned to balance a crafted use of syntax and words with the philosophical to evoke an emotional response in the reader. That is, he learned not to disorient the reader with too much symbolism or sublime emotion, but to write in a poetic voice informed by ordinary language, speaking equally to the intellect and the emotion of the reader. He also learned to avoid using poetic language as a mask to hide behind, but rather as a way to connect with and better understand his world. Under Winters, Islas learned to explore the dense textures of words themselves as they poured from the mouth, vibrated in air, and were registered by the ear and brain. Islas applied Winters's theory of "unity of form and content," using meter and syntax as a unified grammar to reflect a particular worldview. Islas apprenticed dutifully, writing poetry exercises, keeping notebooks brimming with detailed analyses of other poets' use of meter, rhythm, and tone; he also wrote detailed analyses of individual poems, describing their connotations and how they spoke to the broader context of human consciousness. Islas became a poet with vision and imagination, learning to write poetry that was intense but not overwrought.

Yvor Winters's poetics of rationality helped form Islas's poetic and critical sensibility. Earlier, Islas had read Spanish philosopher-poet George Santayana. As an undergraduate in the late 1950s, Islas often sought solace in Santayana's poems—especially when feeling depressed after discovering that men he had formed crushes on failed to reciprocate his love. And Santayana's turn away from the divine to the body as a site of sensory expression at which to understand our place in the world was particularly attractive to Islas, who had turned away from the church and who wanted to understand his same-sex desire with more clarity. Islas was also drawn to poets and novelists that were keenly aware of the human body—to poets such as Walt Whitman, Federico García Lorca, Ralph Waldo Emerson, Emily Dickinson (even writing a poem in her honor, "In the Manner of E. Dickinson"), and Elizabeth Bishop; and to novelists like Marcel Proust, Colette, D. H. Lawrence, Yukio Mishima, and E. M. Forster. As Islas moved from his undergraduate to graduate studies, and from his interest in Santayana to Winters, he experimented with writing, for example, poems that balanced the powerfully forward-thrusting style of Hart Crane with that of the slow, meditative line of Emerson. He would invent queer, Chicano poet-narrators who balanced philosophical meditation and psychological investigation within traditional sonnet verse structures. In the poem "LIGHT," Islas balanced the self with a Jungian notion of the "God-image" by inventing a fully constituted poet-narrating Self that fails to apprehend its Other: that "golden one who was not ours, / who was not mine" (box 9, folder 16).

Islas admired Denise Levertov for her word-in-the-world sensibility. He felt that she had successfully managed to open up the poetic line in such a way as to combine the pleasure of verse and image with a painful sense of violence present in her everyday world. This was a goal that Islas sought for his own poems. And to this end he did not hesitate to mix low- and high-brow, canonic and popular, cultural expressive forms. Consider, for example, his sexy four-part video-song "Anna, Albertine, Isabel, and Emma" (first names of Western-canonic female characters). And, Islas playfully announced in parentheses alongside these video poems that they were to be recited by twentieth-century gender-bending figures like Boy George and Annie Lennox. Thus, Islas intended to use the video-poem as a glamorous multimedia aesthetic to dramatize a poetics of transvestism that would resonate with the contemporary world.

Islas experimented with a wide variety of poetic strategies. In his poems "Aztec Angel," "Cuauhtémoc's Grave," and "Resident Fellow I," Islas used the *corrido*, or ballad, form, European-identified lyric modes, and a prose-poetic style to take his readers into the hybrid world of Chicano/a subjectivity as shaped by an ever-evolving mix of contemporary and pre-Columbian knowledge systems. In "Resident Fellow I" Islas invented a Chicano poet-narrator with a global reach. This poet-narrator is a border subject looking to turn a profit by transforming pre-Columbian heritage into a commodity to be consumed in the capitalist marketplace. Islas writes, "An Aztec face, red clay, two-fifty / At the Juárez market" (box 32, folder 7). In "Aztec Angel" Islas played with visual form— mixing a horizontal reading of the lines with a cascading verticality—that both mimics the angel's fall and allows the poem to dance vertiginously on the page. Islas also used the technique of linguistic code-switching to suspend the reader somewhere between English and Spanish, between a Mexican-identified culture and a mainstream United States. The poetic line and subject enter into the fluid space of Chicano identity that connects to but is not shackled by a collective past. These more Chicano-identified poems address issues of memory, identity, history, and heritage in order to validate and reclaim a lost Chicano, mestizo history—but not in any sense to delimit Chicano/a subjectivities imaginatively or psychically. Here Islas formed a Chicano poetics that fused Aztec/Nahuatl archetypes with queer Chicano subjectivity—on a personal and interpersonal level— to turn the Chicano object back into a multilingual/sexual inhabiting subject.

Islas's mid-1970s poetry sought an aesthetics of resistance, but not as an essentializing poetics. Certainly, Islas experimented with a *raza* rhetoric such as that found in José Montoya's "El Louie"—a poet-narrator who similarly speaks through linguistic and racial in-between spaces to wedge in and break up the hegemonic language systems—but not to a racially exclusive degree. Islas also experimented with a poetic voice much like Gloria Anzaldúa's, which plays with heteronormative behavioral codes.[12] By crafting an overt same-sex poetics, Islas further stretched the limits of the kind of traditionally macho Chicano poetics seen in, for example, Rodolfo Gonzales's "Yo soy Joaquín/I am Joaquin."

Between 1973 and 1978, after years of writing poems informed by a Wintersian poetics of rationality, Islas came into his own poetically. Not entirely coincidentally, this was also when Islas attained a politicized identity as queer and Chicano. In "Faggots," a poem written toward the end of that period, Islas invented a poet-narrator that powerfully collapses the homophobic present with the equally homophobic but more barbaric past:

> We were slaughtered
> And sent here to be consumed
> (Hermaphrodites burn well.)
>
> Our condition, assume the eaters,
> Is transitory and remedial,
> Passing through them as we do
> For their nourishment or indigestion.
>
> Some of us sparkle and melt
> In fires that grow hotter,
> Die down quietly
> Or in a hiss of steam
> Muffled by dampness and fog,
> Our traces, woodsy, stale odors
> Mixed with the blood and droppings
> Of vermin, the kind of late November smoke
> That sticks to clothes and furniture.
>
> Others hang out in warehouses,
> Stripped and beheaded,
> Dripping row upon row, hooked,
> Bumping into each other at 3 and 4 a.m.
> Limbs labeled, packaged and sent out
> To the best and worst places in town,
> Morsels to be savored, gristle trimmed away.
>
> A few, the privileged,
> Are used to start the fire,
> Kindling for those worthy to be called
> Criminal and Heretic.
> Hence the name: faggot.
>   Faggot.
> In America, "queer" and "cocksucker"
> Are the dirtiest words.
>
>   "Hey fag, where you goin', fag?
>   How come you limpin', fag?"
>   "Cause he just got laid."

They have no matches,
Only rocks and beercans;
A couple wear crosses round their necks.
(box 9, folder 11)

The poet-narrator takes the reader as far back as the middle-ages: to the
time of the Inquisition, and to Dante, who depicts Satan cannibalizing
bodies at the end of the Inferno: there has been little progress or enlight-
enment in the struggle against homophobia.

This period also coincided with the deep self-loathing and suicidal
self-doubt that grew from Islas's tumultuous romance with Jay Spears—
his "muse." After living together for three years in the early 1970s, Jay
Spears decided that the monogamous domestic life was not for him; he
actively sought out a lifestyle that, at least at first, went counter to Islas's
more domestic inclination. Spears wanted to indulge in a post-Stonewall,
queer emancipated S&M sex and drug scene; Islas wanted to build a nest.
The poems inspired by and reflective of this period are among Islas's
best. In them, concision of poetic form combines with a culturally signif-
icant iconographic imagery that expresses an erotics of pain and pleasure
in a relationship between the poet-narrator and a Jay Spears–like figure.
One such untitled poem reads:

If I was to disobey . . .

If I was to disobey my father,
    Would his machismo capture me
        in his net to keep me obedient?
If I told him I had a mind of my own . . .
    I didn't think Blacks were bad . . .
    talking to a guy didn't mean I wasn't a virgin . . .
        (because I am)
    going with the guys on an overnight demonstration . . .
would he tighten that net to keep
        my mind obedient?
    papa, mine, please be kind
            because
    If you catch me in your net of
        restriction and protection

        I'll fight back
            because
                I'm human.

        My mind is mine
                these things aren't bad
        You feel this way/you make me sad.
    If I was to dishonor my father,
            would his machismo disregard me as his daughter?
    Do grades mean the world to you?
            Does my white marriage also?
            If you disregaurded me, my father,
                    my love
    Which can disregaurd/has disregaurded
            those moments of your

                treatment of me as an object
            not human
        (box 28, folder 6)

In another poem, addressed implicitly to Jay and titled "Motherfucker or the Exile" (box 11, folder 4), Islas gives a Catholic twist to the Icarus myth, addressing himself to the Father and weighing the transcendent figure down with the heavy chains of S&M. One stanza reads,

    Father, I need your hand. Tie my ankles
    And wrists or I will soar into extinction.
    Chain me to bedposts and whip me for my sins
    (box 11, folder 4)

Islas transformed his experiences with Jay—and Islas's own S&M encounters—into an empowered queer Chicano poetic voice that revisits and controls the pain of both his past (his father and the Catholic Church) and his present (Jay's rejection). In other poems written during this period, Islas often laced the sensual with a destructive ingredient. In his poem "Mishima," for example, God is a trinity made up of "Waiting, disavowal, fetishism" (box 9, folder 12), and any form of sensual intimacy is transformed into a bloody bath of bodily collisions. In "For J.E.S," Islas invents a poet-narrator who gives flesh to the disembodied and secularizes the sacred to hold at bay his sexual desire for an unattainable love object:

> Oh, my angel, your thigh sliding under mine,
> Loins, pungent and earthly, do not create
> the yearning for another time, another place.
> *(box 11, folder 4)*

There is another element to Islas's injecting the profane into the sacred here. This was not only about clearing a space where traditional patterns of behavior would fall to the side (religious ideology, say) but also about Islas's inventing poet-narrators who desire whiteness—the Jay Spears figure who appears throughout these poems as "golden," angelic, and white. Here, Islas's poet-narrator is not only sexualized, but racialized, desiring to penetrate and inhabit a body he can never have.

Islas also invented poet-narrators who speak in many different voices not only to convey the complexity of desire as caught up in a white/brown erotic dialectic, but, in the Wintersian tradition, to energize the poem by yoking together the emotive and rational at the level of content and form. In the poem "Desire," for example, Islas used enjambment to dramatize the power behind the emotions carried by each line (box 11, folder 4). Islas constructed the poem so that visually the lines would spill over the edge of the stanzas, or what Islas identified as boxed rooms. Here, Islas invented a poet-narrator who cruises from room to room where different lines and voices represent line-ups of possibilities that are ultimately mutually exclusive.[13] In a letter, Diane Middlebrook remarks of this poem, "You *subsume* a significant history; yet that history can't be known except syllable by syllable"; she also describes how his poetry walks a liminal line between the "waking life" and "dreaming," where the poet captures "the glower of things to come forward into time" (undated note; box 9, folder 11). This is one of the many forms Islas used to explore the seen/unseen, conscious/unconscious, absence/presence dialectics of same-sex desire.

Islas often used the trope of the transvestite to complicate otherwise reductive ontologies and epistemologies. He shared this device not only with Bishop's cross-dressed poetics, but also with the Chicano *rasquache* sensibility (an innovative recycling of old forms and images). Unlike the Wintersian poetics of rationality, which aimed to balance reason and emotion, Islas's *rasquache* poetic actively juxtaposed traditionally divided spaces (Spanish vs. English, Western canonical vs. Chicano non-canonical, straight vs. queer) to make apparent how such divisions work to segregate bodies and subjectivities.[14] For example, in his poem "Blueboy," blueberries, a yellow rose, hand prints on buttocks, Hieronymus Bosch, and D. H. Lawrence make for a textured *rasquache* aesthetics that emplaces a queer Chicano sensibility (box 11, folder 4). In his poem "Ambush," he invented a poet-narrator who cruises S&M clubs only to discover Priapus, the Greek god of fertility:

> In this red light, Priapus lies in wait
> And hunts for assholes;
> Or, barring Him, fingers and fists
> Will do the trick
>
> *(box 11, folder 4)*

And in the already mentioned poem "Motherfucker or the Exile," Islas's poet-narrator alludes to the snake-tailed, many-headed dog of Greek mythology, Cerberus. Islas's Cerberus, however, does not guard the gates to Hades but is a bouncer at an S&M club. And in "Bondage and Discipline" Islas invested his queer-identified poet-narrator with the power to cause pain, but this time as a process of self-healing: on a literal rack, the poet-narrator wrenches from deep cavities within his psyche those destructive patterns of inherited dysfunctional familial behavior (box 11, folder 4).

Islas's writing from this period also coincided with his heavy use of alcohol and drugs. Often, Islas used these as themes for his poetry. In the poem "Moonshine," Islas created a soaked-in-a-scotch-haze poet-narrator who does not pen a Hallmark ode to love on Valentine's day (February 14, 1977; box 11, folder 4), but plays instead with *spirited* double entendres: "moonshine" (alcohol and night) and "lunatic" (moon and crazy). The poet-speaker announces,

> I am the moon now.
> In the windows, cold and indifferent,
> I gaze at myself and the people.
> They're usually drunk.

The poet morphs into the moon, *luna,* then the *luna*tic, multiplying himself as he stares, drunk, at his own reflection. Poetry became a space in which Islas could exercise self-control in public by externalizing the chaos of the private.

Much of Islas's poetry was unpublished in his day, for he was plagued by feelings of insecurity concerning his talent in this domain. He only sent a few poems out to be reviewed by literary journals. And in spite of the massive corpus that he produced (now brought together in Aldama 2003), he never published a collection of poems. Near the end of his life, he made the melancholy remark, "Many of my poems sit in my drawer. They are too depressing to publish" (interview, *Stanford Daily,* February 20, 1990).

OTHER WRITERLY SELVES

Islas's practice of the Wintersian poetics of rationality spilled over into his novel writing; it also spilled over into his journal entries, epistles, and autobiographical accounts. Islas was very much aware of his private writing as public performance; all of his letters and journal entries mix fact with fiction in a stylized mode to appeal to the mind and emotion and also to blur the boundary between private document and fictional endeavor. In one of his journal entries Islas invented an older sibling for himself, Beto, who dies as an infant and buries their father's affections with him in the grave. Biographically, Islas was the firstborn, so this journal entry-turned-fictional tale became a narrative for him to work through issues with his father in the "privacy" of the journal entry. This is to say that Islas's private life was self-consciously constructed. His private self was itself a spectacle.

Islas's ease with crossing borders—fact into fiction, private into public and vice versa—came from living a life at the social margins. To survive at Stanford, he masked his queerness in a largely straight, white-populated public sphere. Even when he turned to alcohol and drugs, he knew how to negotiate the private (his gin-and-tonic soaked inner turmoil and grief) with a smooth veneer of public polish and composure. Islas was fundamentally afraid of exposing his faults and weaknesses to a world he felt might bite back. To this end, he never improvised, not even with his lecture notes. He typed out his lectures in fully formed sentences, paragraphs, and arguments to read as he stood before his class.

To survive, Islas became a bridge-patroller who would control movements between the public and the private. To this end, he used language to assert control within a discursive economy of queer, Chicano surveillance. He learned to say certain things in certain ways and not others. So while his more private writings might at first glance seem to give the sense of the true, inner Islas, in actuality they usually enact an impulse of artful self-invention. Islas blurred the lines between the creative and the artifactual in his letters and journals to dispel hierarchies of difference. Both were sites of textual pleasure for Islas. For example, in an entry titled "Notes for a letter to Jim Paulsen," Islas used the narrative technique of the second-person address to recreate a conversation with his psychologist, Dr. Paulsen. Here, Islas's writing had both a public and a private element. He used figurative language and metaphors with the gaze of a reader in mind; but he also worked through private conflicts about being with Jay and being at Stanford, seeing both as white patriarchal entities that would dehumanize and leave queer Chicano subjects "out of their game."

Islas wrote to different audiences, both in private and public, to perform different identities and to control private/public frames and discursive flows. To his family he would want to be read as more quietly gay identified; to his lovers he would want to be read as more visibly gay. (Islas's young lover, Eric, wrote him in mid-1960s: "You have shown me a very beautiful attitude towards sex"; box 2, folder 4.) At other times Islas would construct narratives that would play up his identification as Chicano. And he would sometimes perform scripts that would allow him to be read as the alienated university professor. Of course, different contexts called for different performances. Islas used a meta-testimonial technique to frame the private as public and to foreground identity as performance. We see this clearly in his autobiographical/memoir "The Loneliest Man in the World," where Islas used the epistolary genre to frame the story of the narrator's (a thinly disguised Islas) coming to terms with his own outlawed sexuality, his relationship with a destructive father, and a student's death from an AIDS-related disease (box 9, folder 17). As with his poetry and novels, here Islas controlled the movement between fact and fiction, epistolary and autobiographical form to texture a world where heteromasculine-identified insecurities lead to destructively patterned relationships that systematically and violently force hierarchies of difference—straight versus queer, sinner versus saint, whore versus virgin—onto a range of experiential possibility.

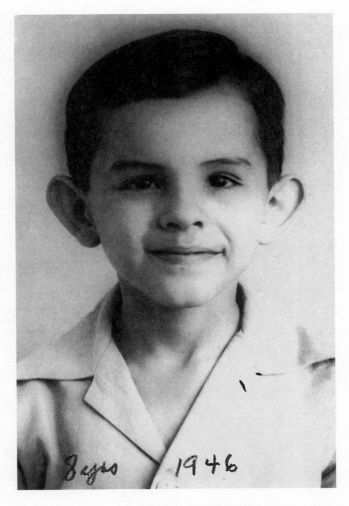

Islas ("Sonny") in 1946, the year he contracted the polio virus.

Islas, 1956 (college graduation portrait).

Islas during graduate school at Stanford.

Islas, 1971, begins to teach at Stanford and to explore his sexuality.

Islas's paternal grandmother, Crecenciana (Mama Chonita), a
schoolteacher.

Islas's maternal grandfather, Conrado La Farga, whom he never knew.

Islas's mother, Jovita La Farga, at age seventeen.

Islas's father, Arturo Islas Sr., standing outside their house in El Segundo barrio in El Paso.

Islas walking with his grandmother Crecenciana (Mama Chonita) in El Paso.

Islas's high school in El Paso.

Islas's study at his parents' house, where he wrote the novel *La Mollie and the King of Tears*.

THREE Sexuality

Arturo Islas's sense of himself as a sexual being underwent dramatic transformations as he moved through a variety of social, cultural, and historical spaces: He came of age as a Mexican American in El Paso during a conservative early 1950s. He began to discover his same-sex desire within a co-ed segregated and draconian-ruled Stanford campus. He struggled to open closet doors during a queer-phobic yet heterosexual-revolutionary 1960s. He forced those same closet doors open during the 1970s only to close them again during the queer-oppressive 1980s. Islas spent a lifetime struggling with an array of conflictive and confusing feelings that gravitated around his sense of freedom and constraint as a man coming into his gay sexuality at a time when tectonic shifts in sexual politics and expression were taking place.

EARLY DAYS

Arturo Islas was a sensitive child who did not identify with his father's macho role model. Instead, he would experience moments of forbidden sensual pleasure when his father was off at work, dancing the jitterbug in his mother's skirts and abandoning himself to the smells and darkness of her closet. (He fictionalizes some of these experiences in *The Rain God*, where his narrator describes Islas's fictional counterpart, Miguel Chico, as finding refuge in the "familiar smells and darkness" of his mother's closet, which "kept him company and faintly reassured him" [17]). As a child, Islas disassociated himself from his father, who appeared to him as brutish and indifferent to sensory stimuli. Instead, he identified with his mother, who often held Islas and paid attention to sensual textures (clothing, makeup, and perfumes) that appealed to Islas. However, Islas's early impulse to move toward the soft, vibrant, sentimental world of women—not just his mother, but also their maid, María Ramírez—met with a series of obstacles. As he grew older, he realized that abandoning himself to his imagination and senses—cross-dressing in the privacy of his parents' room when alone in the house, playing in closets, or playing cutout dolls with the maid—was, in the eyes of the father, wrong for a little boy. As far as the father was concerned, this kind of behavior in a boy was more than strange; it would certainly lead him astray sexually, so he severely reprimanded and punished Islas whenever he caught him, telling him that he would grow up to be a *joto* if he continued. Only later would Islas come to understand his father's homophobia, largely Arturo Sr.'s way of distancing himself from something that he feared was very close to home: as much as he tried to ignore the fact, he knew that his brother Carlos was closeted gay. Islas Sr. feared that his young son's cross-dressing proclivity might foretell things to come: another *joto* and sexual deviant in the Islas family.

As Islas grew from child to young boy, the women who had originally encouraged his transgressively feminine imaginative play began to discourage it. Even his mother, who tended to indulge Islas, did not want to see her son playing with cutout dolls and dressing in skirts. Young Islas, able to read and fully immersed in his elementary school and library's worlds of discovery, sought alternative imaginative means of exploring polymorphous sensual and bodily cravings. Reading, he discovered, was an imaginative outlet. Islas learned to read well before his classmates largely because of his paternal grandmother's daily after-school instruction. With reading, he accessed a new set of playthings and worlds: the rich textual offerings and new relational possibilities to be found between book covers. Though his father disliked young Islas's affinity for reading books (especially novels), as this was in his mind a very feminine activity, he tolerated it because of his strong belief in education. The young Islas was thus free to live vicariously as a woman being romanced or a man romancing without incurring his father's disapproval.

As a teenager, Islas's well-fed imaginative appetites became an asset. In high school, his natural empathy, enhanced by years of reading and relating to the more sensitive, feminine, parent, in combination with his good looks, made him especially attractive to the opposite sex. Not only did he know how to speak and listen to girls with a deep sensitivity, but he could dance high school social favorites like the jitterbug with dazzling dexterity. (He loved to dance with his mother, practicing and honing his skill as a dancer in the privacy of his home.) Unlike his fraternal peers, he was not afraid of the opposite sex; rather, he related to them deeply. This was, of course, the early 1950s, when dating was either a group activity or involved going to the hop or school dance, where sexual expression was limited to hand holding and, at most, chaste kissing. Islas could date Mexican American, Anglo, and Jewish girls at his high school without feeling any conflict about his sexuality; this would happen later, in college, when Islas realized that his true feelings and attractions were for men. One of his high school sweethearts was Harriet ("Holly") Gladstein, a tall, popular blonde young woman who, even after he came out later in life, would remain very dear to Islas. On more than one occasion Islas would say that, had he been straight, he would have married her—and had a much less complicated life. In high school, then, Islas could perform the well-spoken and dashing romantic young man he had gleaned from novels and yet be safe from straight sexual encounters. He had yet to enter a social world where he would have to face coming to terms with a desire that did not fit a heterosexual mold.

When Islas entered Stanford as a freshman in 1956, the sociosexual context and attendant expectations were radically different. He now lived twenty-four hours a day, seven days a week, on a strictly segregated campus, and he found himself pulled in two directions: he was surrounded by young men he found himself increasingly attracted to, and at the same time the dating stakes were higher. Dating girls was expected and so, too, was more sexual contact. This campus that policed borders between the male and female populations ironically encouraged Islas to spend time in the company of young men—men that would more and more spark his desire. At the same time, the pressures of campus dating life were making it clear that courting women went against his true desires. At the same time that he found himself physically attracted to his male companions, he needed to perform heterosexuality to appear "normal" in the eyes of those male companions.

At a co-ed Stanford campus in the mid to late 1950s, Islas began to experience a conflict and clash of romantic feelings and desires. He yearned for physical intimacy and to express his love, but the young men surrounding him only spoke of women. By the time Islas entered his senior year at Stanford, he had experienced several deep crushes and disappointments with male friends. He often fell in love with them from afar, afraid to articulate his love for fear of being labeled perverse and becoming an outcast. Islas above all wanted to feel like he belonged. (Of course, this fear of being socially alienated was amplified by an already deeply felt insecurity in regard to being a racial minority on campus.) Mostly, Islas dared speak his forbidden love only in the pages of his journals. However, there were times when he felt it safe to express his love to those male "friends" that he thought reciprocated and with whom he dared to cross the heteronormative line. These intimate friendships always led to deep disappointment. Love affairs were short-lived and considered by Islas's love interests to be merely a last phase of boyhood before entering the adult world of heterosexual coupling, marriage, and children. After returning from Christmas vacation, Islas experienced one such disappointment when Jim, whom he had fallen for before the break, gave him the cold shoulder. In his journal, Islas writes of his disappointment; he saw "Jim twice today" but Jim did not acknowledge him. He continues,

"I think he saw me right away, but I turned to look out of the window so that he would not feel compelled to sit next to me. Perhaps it was so that he would not see that I wanted him to sit next to me. Jim is very perceptive in some ways. He did look at me for some long seconds" (January 13, 1959; box 53, folder 1). Islas understood the need to be discrete, but did not understand Jim's outright rejection of him. Like his other male friendships, this one too ended with Islas stealing furtive glances and repressing his desire and Jim deliberately shutting him out by avoiding all contact. He writes, "I was able to see the back of his head—sometimes willingly, other times accidentally, always afraid that he might sense how much I have missed whatever understanding (if any) there is between us" (January 13, 1959).

Inhabiting a homophobic, sexually surveillanced 1950s college campus, Islas had to keep his sexual identity in the closet. His moments of intimacy with men were few and far between and could never be acknowledged by either Islas or his love interests for fear of social ostracism. Even writing in his journal was a dangerous act because Islas lived in dormitories with roommates, so, even here, one gets the sense that his expressions of male-male love are covert. Islas was aware that even his most private thoughts could be used against him if someone was to read his journal. So, he often wrote between the lines and played down much of his interest in male-male intimacies. Though his journals proved an important space for him to understand from a slight emotional remove his pangs of love, above all Islas knew to protect his place as a Mexican American scholarship student within this space of privilege that could easily be taken from him. Islas never came out and made visible his deep friendship with students like Jim, but he did write of the pain he felt after these different love interests rejected what he referred to as his "gift" (his love).

Jim and the other love interests Islas writes about in his journals were of a particular physical and emotional type: athletic, emotionally distant, middle-class Anglo men. (All of the men Islas became involved with later in life would fit this type.) This male type represented everything that Islas was not: Islas grew up a Mexican American, which put him at the margins of a largely Anglo society. He grew up physically disabled. He grew up identifying with a sentimental, emotionally expressive mother. Not surprisingly, then, when Islas formed crushes as an undergraduate, they were on men who were his exact opposite and who promised to fulfill all that he lacked. Of course, this was precisely the type that would reject Islas's warm, loving advances. In many ways, Islas desired men who were not only like his father—good looking and emotionally distant—but who would remind him of his own limitations and cause him pain. At one point he insightfully identifies this self-destructive behavior as a "self-inflicted isolation" that he likens to "self-abuse," concluding that "the concrete remains irreconcilable to the intention" (June 5, 1959). Driven by this self-destructive impulse, he would experience himself more and more acutely as a sexually, racially, and physically diseased other.

Through the rest of his senior year at Stanford, Islas continued to very delicately pursue men; most of these attempts ended in rejection and with Islas blaming himself either for not being straight or for not being good enough. He writes, "I guess I don't look 'the type.' I've been jealous of *that* type all my life" (January 16, 1959; box 53, folder 1). After a series of such disappointments, Islas desperately tried to be "normal," so he went out on a date with a young woman he liked. He tried hard to do what he had heard the other boys talk about: feeling her body and kissing her. As he wrote in his journal, this experience only reminded him of how he wanted to be seduced and physically devoured by a man: "What's more wonderful than to give one's body when one realizes the significance of the act and the shamelessness of acceptance?" (January 16, 1959). Ironically, his going out on a date only solidified in Islas's mind his own yearning to be with men: he could identify with the woman, but never desired to be with a woman. He sought out women and their company, yet he knew that he desired "men's *bodies* and not their souls," as he recollects of this period later in life (June 30, 1987; box 2, folder 1). Not only did his attempt at heterosexual college dating fail to "cure" him of desiring men, it reminded him of his difference, flooding him with nausea and self-hatred. He considered suicide, but resisted this extreme expression of self-hatred. His journal, in fact, served as a therapeutic place for Islas to work out his intense feelings of self-loathing. At one point, he identifies his journal as "an impersonal void" (January 30, 1959) that allowed him to redirect his pain onto a society that wrongfully outlawed same-sex desire and sensibility.

In several journal entries, he concludes that there is no harm in being gay because no harm is done to others or to the world. His early religious indoctrination, however, would resurface and overpower his objective evaluation of his desire for men, transforming the journal space from refuge to prison. After being rejected by another young man, Larry, Islas envisions himself a "sinner" who must do penance to cleanse his soul for being, he self-reflects, "impure throughout [his] life" (March 10, 1959; box 53; folder 1). Here, Islas would slip into a saint/sinner paradigm, reading his desire as perverse and a sin against the church. If he did not somehow change his "nature," he would be damned. On this particular occasion, he did not wish to kill himself or become magically heterosexual, but rather to kill of his desire altogether. He imagined himself living the life of a celibate monk, devoted not so much to the church, but to his studies. However, toward the end of his senior year, he realized that this was no answer. He remarks, "One cannot live on memories or books or even music" (May 7, 1959; box 53, folder 1).

Stanford during the late 1950s proved a painful place for Islas to come of age sexually. Even when he found like-desiring men, he was haunted by the dominant, heteronormative ideology. Islas wanted to affirm his feelings for men but knew that such love had no place in his society. He vacillated between unreasoned self-hatred and a more reasoned understanding of his sexual preference. He knew, too, that he could not repress or squash his desire. Finally, he settled for the understanding that he would "hate it and love it at the same time" (August 2, 1959). Islas's love/hate understanding of his sexuality forced him to learn to walk those shadowed lines between straight and queer in order not to risk complete ostracism, which in his mind was akin to self-annihilation. It would be some time before Islas could begin to pull apart and work through his complex sense of sexual and bodily being in the world.

NEW BEGINNINGS

In June 1960, Islas graduated from Stanford with a BA, firmly convinced that he would spend the rest of his days loving and hating himself for being gay. However, when he returned to Stanford to begin his studies for a PhD that fall, campus life and the culture at large were beginning to explode at the seams, offering a glimmer of new sexual possibilities. Islas was no longer an undergraduate bound exclusively to the campus, with its nightly curfews; and the fifties, with its suffocating sociosexual conservatism, was over. While Islas was in graduate school, he lived through a period of tremendous shifts—especially with regard to the gay/lesbian communities in nearby San Francisco. The power that was growing among those that had been labeled sexual "deviants" was shaking up stale institutional structures and conservative moral attitudes in San Francisco and New York. By the time Islas was in the fifth year of his PhD program, the urban centers in the United States were exploding with proactive sexual politics and the open expression of eroticisms that challenged the rigid heteronormativity of the 1950s.[1]

The Stanford campus was changing dramatically, too. In December 1965, the administration finally recognized the Stanford Sexual Rights Forum—the earliest known national student group to advocate the civil rights of gays and lesbians. (This became fully institutionalized in 1970 with the opening of the Lesbian, Gay, and Bisexual Community Center.) By the mid to late 1960s, societal attitudes toward gays and lesbians had changed radically from a decade earlier. Due to local and national political efforts, people were more aware of the history of injustices leveled at gays and lesbians. In this new climate, Islas was more at ease with his gay sexuality and was meeting men who were not afraid to consummate their sexual desire. He was at last free to explore the emotions of having same-sex relationships. The first to deeply affect him was a relationship with Edward Bergh—an artist and a student of architecture at Stanford. Islas fell in love with Ed Bergh and by 1967 they were living together in a rented house in Palo Alto. Bergh offered Islas stability in a topsy-turvy, homophobic world. Together they created a safe space where they could grow together and pursue their careers. While Islas studied for his PhD, Bergh worked toward his degree in architecture and played the household handyman: tiling their bathroom, repairing windows, even fixing their car. Islas kept this life secret from his parents—he and Bergh lived together as "roommates"—knowing that while the sociosexual mores of San Francisco and Palo Alto might be changing for the better, those of his family back in El Paso certainly had not. In fact, the town's homophobia hit home viscerally when its media unsympathetically portrayed his uncle Carlos's murder as a gay sexual tryst gone wrong. That Islas's father distanced himself and his family from the incident and from Carlos was an indication to Islas that the moment to come out to his parents would have to wait.

For the most part, Islas and Bergh realized their dream—to live a normal, domestic life together. However, within this gay-affirming domestic space, Islas's childhood demons haunted him, and deep-seated behavioral patterns would surface and eventually destroy their relationship. Islas assumed the role of the father: the emotionally reserved, selfish taker. Bergh assumed the role of the mother: the sentimental, giving nurturer. Islas's love was selfish and non-monogamous; Bergh's love was selfless and singular. At one point Bergh writes Islas, "I truly believe and feel that I love you, not with a love that is locked about you but with a love that is broad, that at moments caresses you with all that I can feel as intimate from the depths of my being, that at other moments seem not there, but ever present, waiting as with undulating sea to be with you again and once again and . . . all under the golden sun" (undated note, box 2, folder 2). Islas could not handle this selfless love, rejecting Bergh as he slipped more and more into playing the role of the tyrant at home and having random sexual encounters with other men. Islas played the tyrant, often verbally abusing and degrading Bergh as his father had done to his mother and as he himself had done to his younger brother Mario. Bergh played his part well, performing the victim role by complaining to Islas constantly of his physical ailments like his "burning stomach" and "coated tongue," which he said were a consequence of Islas's abusive behavior. As the years passed, Islas and Bergh stayed together, role-playing the tyrant/victim dyad more and more. By the early 1970s, their relationship was near its end. Islas had become an emotionless narcissist who brought home his lovers to remind Bergh of his distaste for commitment; and Bergh sank deeper and deeper into physical illness. Within this environment, Islas became the monster he most feared in his father. Bergh finally ended the relationship, and on March 30, 1973, he writes Islas a farewell note: "I'm tired of being dumped on! . . . I'm tired of your whining and complaining; of your 'put-downs'; of your beseeching others to constantly do things for you. . . . I'm tired of not being able to expect 'love making,' at least once in awhile" (box 2, folder 2). Islas and Bergh broke off a relationship Islas describes in his journal as "interminable, masochistic, like the grating of the nerves" (November 30, 1973; box 2, folder 2). Ironically, Islas had transformed a long-yearned-for gay safe-space into a site of dysfunction, sabotaging his own dreams of a healthy and loving gay relationship.

QUEER (IN)VISIBILITY

By the mid-1960s, Islas had witnessed a dramatic transformation in the sociosexual climate, both locally and nationally. The many "outlawed" voices that were being heard loudly across the nation empowered Islas to re-view his otherwise conflicted sense of sexual self. He no longer had to identify as a "deviant" just because he desired men. This is not to say that Islas was suddenly liberated as a same-sex erotic self. This was only the beginning of a visible gay/lesbian struggle to fight denigrating stereotypes and homophobic injustices. Islas still had to be careful, for most still harbored a deep homophobia, including his more liberal colleagues. Outside of the more progressive campuses like Stanford and its neighbor, Berkeley, and outside urban centers like New York City and San Francisco, conservatism still reined. Islas knew, for example, that sex education textbooks still identified nonprocreative sex as morally perverse. He was also acutely aware of the deeply ingrained homophobia in the fields of medicine, law, and the humanities. Of course, homophobia was still very much present in his hometown and within his family. Islas feared coming out to his parents—especially his father. And after he learned that Uncle Carlos's murderer was found not guilty—the law determined that he was justly defending himself as the victim of a perverse sex crime—Islas was filled with anger and discouragement. The mid-1960s was certainly a period of change, but it was also marked with conflictive feeling. Islas could more openly explore his sexuality and live with a partner like Ed Bergh, but at the same time he was acutely aware of the violent homophobia that continued to erupt around him. For Islas, the idea that the world had become more tolerant was an illusion, preferring to see men, he writes, "hurt each other [rather] than allow them to love each other" (Norman Mailer lecture; box 25, folder 6). Though much had changed, Islas knew that he would have to be careful in a world populated by the kind of white, homophobic males that had "sat on the grand jury that investigated the murder of my uncle" (Norman Mailer lecture). Not surprisingly, in spite of his empowered sense of sexuality during this period, Islas stayed in the closet to his family, his colleagues, and to many of his friends for most of his life.

By the time Islas had finished his PhD and begun his tenure-track job at Stanford in 1971, the 1960s era of resistance (the anti–Vietnam War protests, the brown and black power movements, and the Stonewall riots, for example) had opened up new doors for exploring an otherwise marginalized identity. In the spirit of sexual liberation and experimentation, Islas moved away from wanting to fulfill his sexual appetites through a domestic, monogamous partnering. This is not entirely surprising. Islas, after all, lived in a sexually emancipated San Francisco where then-democratic assemblyman Willy Brown passed progressive legislation that legalized "homosexuality" and certain "unnatural acts" in private between consenting adults. So, as Islas broke up with Ed Bergh, he began frequenting more often San Francisco's bathhouses and cruising San Francisco's South of Market streets, bookstores, and clubs for quick, anonymous sexual trysts. In one journal entry that reflects Islas's sexual experiences in the 1970s he writes that he needed to have as much sex as possible "in order to prove that I *can* act like any other healthy, normal person" (November 10, 1977; box 53, folder 4). So, during the day Islas would don a suit and tie to wear the professor look at Stanford and at night he would wear the leather queen look in San Francisco's S&M clubs. During the day he indulged the mind. At night he indulged the flesh: anonymous and multiple sex encounters, bondage and discipline—and amyl nitrate to enhance the sensual textures.

Islas learned to negotiate two radically different worlds, making sure that the professional and personal would never intersect. The San Francisco gay scene was worlds apart from the largely straight, white, homophobic Stanford scene, where the sociosexual opening of the 1960s was more apparent than real. Coming out as gay—and a sexually experimenting leather queen at that—would certainly have had Stanford colleagues, students, trustees, and the administration up in arms. The formal acceptance of the gay/lesbian caucus on campus did not magically make homophobia disappear. *Stanford Directions*, a university magazine, ran articles that damned the presence of gays and lesbians on campus and that promoted the free use of American Indian icons and names as college athletic team symbols. Islas cut out one such clipping: "Shouldn't Stanford promote the dignity of its students, rather than permitting the organization of a group which promotes sexual deviancy?" (June 1974; box 28, folder 6). And on another occasion, an article in the Stanford publication *California Living Magazine* identified the bathhouses that Islas frequented as "specimens of rotten tissue" that must be excised from a diseased body politic, or we would witness the "accelerating decay [and] decline of civilization" (October 5, 1975; box 28, folder 6). As far as the straight, homophobic population at Stanford was concerned, mechanisms of sexual surveillance should remain firmly in place. To satisfy his sexual appetites and to move forward in his career as a professor, Islas had to perform different selves in different public spaces—a skill he'd been perfecting since childhood—to negotiate lines of tension generated by homophobic institutional and societal values and his sexual needs as they crossed but never collided at the site of his body.

Islas often channeled his frustration about living in a homophobic society into his fiction. His fictional worlds became ways to explore different psychological realms—queer versus straight and personal versus professional. In one of Islas's early works he would indict the social hypocrisy of homophobia. For example, in "Día de los muertos" he writes, "Homosexual human beings are not freaks of nature; the history of the race attests to their existence from the beginning of time. Why doesn't anybody say, plainly and simply, that those who take the Bible literally on this or any other issue are idiots? Will a single passage in Leviticus determine the lives of millions? The message of the New Testament seems lost to most in American society: 'Love thy neighbor as thyself.' *No exceptions*. It is the greatest, most difficult, imaginative concept in all of western literature"

("Día"; box 12, folder 1). Islas used his fiction to come to terms with a society that not only saw him as a great peril to the heteromasculine mainstream, but that taught him, he continues, "to loathe his condition [so deeply it] pierces to the heart." Islas also used his early fiction to explore the sexual energy released in his S&M encounters:

> The sucking, fucking noises in the corridor, the stench of amyl, the smell of perfumed crotches and abused assholes, piss and leather, semen, sweat and spit and nicotine piercing the nostrils as the throat gags, oh Lord! hear my prayer. In the darkness, one shadow kneels to receive another, crouches to take what comes, tongue or cock, a lick or a fist or a boot or a tube of flesh indiscriminate in this shady grove. There are no kisses here. Prostrate, the prostate is massaged, fingers, hands and phalluses emerge to be licked clean by waiting, tireless, numberless mouths. IammyfatherIammymotherIam . . . Love, are you here? Anonymity is your name, various, fluid, insatiable, always in pursuit, the nose catching the scent, turning the head against its will, long since lost, away from what asks or needs or wants or is responsible. Yes, you are here, but where? The silky, hairless testicle in the mouth, the bittersweet of the anus scrubbed clean in anticipation; it hurts to penetrate, it comes halfway there. In revenge, the cock pounds against the back of the throat despite the gagging. Love, you are here, choking, heaving, the Other's flesh ravaging your mouth. I'm on my knees, Lord, have mercy on me. Teach me love. ("Día")

In the fictional re-creation of his S&M experience, Islas explored how he could strip himself bare of mechanisms that traditionally regulated his sexual desires, actions, and possible identities. In both the fiction and the actual S&M experience, Islas cleared space for self-affirmation and agency. He delighted in the mindless pleasures of the rectum and penis, which, in the "simple act of placing another's penis in one's mouth or ass without regard to who is on top or who is on the bottom," love, courting, and sexual position are revealed to be experientially restrictive—mere ideological constructs. On another occasion, Islas writes in his journal of a post–S&M encounter when he goes home with a man named Dennis, gets high on "much amyl" and "grass," and then indulges in a threesome that he describes as "a long, wonderful sexual encounter" (December 19, 1976; box 53, folder 4). In the act of giving and receiving pleasure anonymously to countless bodies to maximize the erotic possibilities, for Islas

fact informed fiction, and fiction informed fact. His fiction, sexual exper-
imentation, and leather queen S&M play enabled him to defy (at least
momentarily) the laws that policed his body in the public sphere. In S&M
and in writing, he discovered spaces where he could experience mo-
ments of pleasure in otherwise forbidden erotic zones.

Islas knew that in his lifetime he would never see a world that would
embrace his sexuality. So rather than try to change a world that had al-
ready damned him as a perverse, deviant, monster, he continued to ex-
plore his many selves in the only space that would allow this: his S&M
play and the fiction in which he replayed it; he would return again and
again to the S&M scene, in his poetry and even in his posthumously pub-
lished *La Mollie and the King of Tears*. Both would become experimental
spaces that allowed him to channel his anger and frustration toward a
homophobic and racist world—spaces that allowed him to rupture the
veneer of heteronormative social convention and actively come to terms
with his internalized self-loathing as located at the basic register of his
sexualized body. The power of fiction and S&M for Islas meant never
having to apologize for who he was, and, as he wrote in his journal,
"never having to say 'be gentle'" (September 8, 1978; box 53, folder 3).

S&M was more than an erotic space for Islas. Like fiction writing, it
was a venue for Islas to creatively reimagine himself in a number of dif-
ferent roles and as a number of different characters:

> S&M among homosexual males is a substitute or surrogate "virile" activ-
> ity for what among non-homosexual males takes the form of streetfights
> or rough sports. All these dreams of virility: the toughness of the cowboy,
> the training of the young soldier, the impassivity of the cop, the bragging
> of the boxer, the calm of the quarterback, the inexhaustible energy of the
> playboy, the control of the pitcher—all find their counterparts in the gay
> bars across the land. ("Día")

Of course, being able to perform virile roles (the cop, boxer, quarterback,
and so on) was also Islas's moment of being able to reverse the racialized
subject position of the Chicano, who is traditionally acted upon and not
allowed to be the agent of his acts. S&M erotic play, then, was a way for
Islas to externalize memories that etched deeply into his body a fear of

rejection and disapproval both as a same-sex desiring body and as a Chicano. Like fiction writing, ritualized S&M allowed him to explore the limits of his racial and sexual place in the world; it provided him with a space in which to exercise his will as a gay Chicano.

S&M worked as a form of therapy for Islas. He enjoyed role-playing the masochistic victim, but he also relished role-playing the sadistic torturer. He associated the victim role both with the Chicano subject position and with his mother; he associated the sadistic role with the Anglo subject position and with his then love interest Jay Spears, as well as with his father. These roles were fluid, and he could go either way. He could role-play the victim/masochist, who is, as he writes in his journal, "in complete control all the while, very much like a bitch who manipulates by appearing passive" (January 20, 1979; box 2, folder 1). He could also perform the sadist: "I do the halter and dog collar with him. His breathing, his action like a dog" (October 30, 1978; box 53, folder 3). Such role-playing allowed him to work through dysfunctional familial patterns of behavior. He knew that his strong identification with his mother's victimhood in opposition to the father's role as the tyrant threatened to limit his erotic freedom. He would role-play either the tyrant/sadist or the victim/masochist in his S&M adventures in San Francisco to explore how they were mutually dependent and created each other—how the masochist exercises control, appearances to the contrary. At one point, he describes his interest in the collaboration between torturer and tortured in S&M that, as he writes, crystallizes at the moment when the "turbulent sessions" transform into a perfect match of "wits and flesh in a fantasy, as if one were able to choose to be a dream figure in another's dream and still remain a dream to oneself" ("Día"). He concludes, "The sex of either does not matter for each assumes ancient, sexless guilts and hoists them onto the scaffolds of Mother and Father."

These acts of shared dreaming in the S&M act allowed Islas to strip his psyche naked and break momentarily free from the dysfunctional role-playing that threatened to take over his present. His acts of discipline and bondage, dominance and humiliation, his use of "chains and footling dildos, fistfucking, whippings mock or actual" were blasphemous acts against the Father—family, church, state—that externalized in a controlled way his deep fear of the father ("Día"). S&M was profoundly liberating for Islas. He often discussed how the moment when violence and sexuality intersect in the S&M ritual would lead to an emancipating space beyond roles of sadist versus masochist, tyrant versus victim, or Chicano versus Anglo that opened into unmapped territories of non-language. (Islas wrote a great deal on S&M, responding both to his own experiences and to other theoretical work like that of Gilles Deleuze; box 9, folder 1.)

S&M was therapeutic for Islas, but only to a point. The role-playing that liberated him from restrictive patterns, he gradually came to see, seemed only to reinforce his dysfunctional relationship with Jay. That Islas could never play the S&M game with Jay only further contributed to the breakdown of their relationship. Jay wanted only to be dominated—and never to dominate. And, Jay didn't want to include Islas in his S&M encounters, which pained Islas, who felt increasingly ostracized and desperate, sinking into an everyday reality in which he played the victim and Jay the tyrant. Islas gradually realized that his S&M ritual transgressions were not helping to empower him with Jay. After an S&M session, he often felt more alienated rather than less. He began to avoid S&M clubs, describing in one journal entry how the different club rooms no longer seemed to invite him to a liberating sexual phantasmagoria, but rather only reminded him of being "excluded from power" in his everyday relationship with Jay (February 25, 1977; box 53, folder 4). He describes in another journal entry how the "slapping of leather, posing, constant activity withheld [was] *not* pleasurable" (April 2, 1977; box 53, folder 4). At night after an S&M session he would wake up and realize that nothing had really changed; that his bruises from beating his "head against the walls" and "weeping without restraint" because of Jay's psychological abuse had not magically disappeared (journal, November 5, 1976; box 53, folder 4).

SADIST AND MUSE

In the fall of 1971, after having recovered from surgeries for ulcerative colitis, Islas met Jay Marion Spears for the first time. Islas was beginning his career as an English professor and Jay was enrolled at the Stanford law school. Islas was immediately drawn to the twenty-one-year-old Jay, whose golden-boy good looks, quick wit, and charm dazzled Islas. However, Islas was still officially with Ed Bergh. A year after meeting Jay, Islas ended his relationship with Ed Bergh and began a heated romance with Jay. By 1973 they were deeply involved—or at least Islas was with Jay. Islas would later recollect that Jay was the first man, "after the operation, 8 years ago," that he had loved (journal, October 20, 1978). Jay was also to be the last great love to enter Islas's life. Even after their roller-coaster ride led them to break up in 1978, Islas expressed in his journal his deep feelings of loss: "I remember the moon and the smell of his body and his golden hair on the pillow" (October 20, 1978; box 53, folder 3). After their breakup Islas continued to fantasize about how they might one day "lie in each other's arms and laugh about these nightmares of past and imposed guilts, lies and limitations. Sex won't be a cruel and dirty joke then—for either of us. Simply itself" (letter; box 2, folder 6).

Jay was also in love with Islas. Their relationship was filled with passion, great sex, and romance. When apart, they would send each other notes and cards dripping in maudlin sentiment: Jay addressed Islas as "Poochie" or as "Odysseus." During their first three years together, they were inseparable, traveling as a couple to places like Spain and France. Islas loved Jay for more than his intellect and Greco-Roman body. He loved Jay because he accepted him despite his imperfect body. When they were naked together for the first time, Islas was touched deeply when Jay reacted with sensitivity and grace at the sight of the piece of gut that protruded from his abdomen, attached to his "shit bag" (colostomy bag). Jay responded similarly to Islas's postoperative sutured anus. Jay's acceptance of Islas in his entirety intensified his love for Jay. Moreover, Islas felt that he had finally met his intellectual equal. He shared his scholarly work and his creative writing with Jay. As far as Islas was concerned, Jay was *the one* for life. In a honeymoon-like mood, they moved in together in a house in Palo Alto. Islas wrote and prepared to lecture at Stanford while Jay studied for his JD. They led a domestic, blissful life— they learned of one another's habits, likes and dislikes, and would even make a ritual out of going to the yearly Berkeley/Stanford Big Game.

But, when Jay finished his degree and started to practice law, he moved to San Francisco, and the honeymoon came to an abrupt end.

From the day of their first meeting, the younger, less experienced Jay was eager to explore his sexual identity; and this was his first same-sex love affair. By the time Jay got to San Francisco, with its radically changing sexual climate, he was eager to explore and experiment, and he wanted an open relationship with Islas. At first this suited Islas, whose own sexual lifestyle included a penchant for cruising and picking up strangers to turn quick tricks: three-ways, foot-fucking on amyl, and leather bondage games, to name a few. However, as time passed, Islas began increasingly to conflate sex with love. This was in part due to Jay's distancing himself emotionally from the relationship and showing less sexual interest in Islas, who began to think he lacked something that the many others offered. He also began to blame himself for Jay's sexual forays and for excluding him from his S&M adventures.

By the mid-1970s, the relationship had begun to crumble. Islas began to obsess over Jay, which would provoke Jay in turn to put up emotional walls. Islas realized, too, that if he did not work through his psychological baggage—his inherited victim/tyrant patterns—he would simply repeat this dynamic with others. Islas wanted to work through the destructive patterns that were pulling them apart: his obsessive love turned him into the martyr/masochist and Jay into the tyrant/sadist. Jay was not interested. As Islas was apt to do, he turned to his fiction to explore his impossible love, writing how neither his fictional character Miguelito (a thinly veiled Islas) nor Sam (a thinly veiled Jay) could ever be truly intimate because both lived within a society that generated myths either of self-possession (Islas described Sam as the "cowboy riding alone") or of selflessness (he described Miguelito's "fear of solitude"), which in combination made it hopeless "for one man to love another" ("Día").

Meanwhile, Jay's career took off; he moved from San Francisco to clerk in D.C. for the U.S. Supreme Court. Islas's insecurities increased ten-fold and his love turned into a self-destructive obsession: "fear, rage, sense of betrayal, abandonment—all turned inward" (journal, May 3, 1976). He would drink himself to sleep at night and began to seriously entertain different ways of committing suicide: jumping off the Bay Bridge, blowing his brains out, or drowning himself in the Pacific. When Islas flew out to D.C. to visit Jay, he found little to comfort him. He became more and more paranoid that he was missing out on an intimate part of Jay's life, especially after he discovered an empty Crisco can, amyl nitrate, and an accumulation of "ever larger dildos" and "more appurtenances of leather and chains" in Jay's bedroom (journal, July 24, 1978; box 53, folder 3). He continues, "the *things* themselves no longer affect me," but they made him feel that Jay was excluding him from sexual experiences that might have made their relationship stronger.

The sadist/masochist duality wreaked havoc with Islas's emotions during the mid- to late-1970s. In the summer of 1975, Islas took the first of several trips to Kokkomaa Island in Finland to get away from Jay and convalesce with friends Stina and Herant Katchadourian. Islas loved his visits to this island, where he would often seek refuge from an over-wrought emotional life. He often noted that Kokkomaa was an appropriate sanctuary considering that this was the island where the Vikings would bury their dead. Here Islas began to untangle his past (his parents' relationship) and his present (his relationship with Jay). He read fiction about tyrant/victim relationships, analyzed his dreams, and talked and wrote about his relationship with Jay. On one occasion, he writes of waking from a nightmare in which he alternately turned, on the one hand, violently angry toward his mother and, on the other hand, both fearful of and desiring toward Jay, who appears in the dream as "cold, uncaring, almost immobile" ("The island: summer 75"; box 2, folder 1). In another dream, he saw a phone cord stretched from El Paso to Palo Alto; he decrypts this as the umbilical cord that kept him attached to dysfunctional relationship patterns between mother and father: "I walk up to [Jay] and ask 'Is there someone else?' 'No,' he answers. We are kneeling on wet rugs. . . . I hit J. with the telephone cord once and sharply. . . . As soon as we are in the apartment I begin to weep without restraint. Before the others come into the living room, Jay says something like, 'I hope you're happy now that you've exposed us' " ("The island: summer 75"). Islas worked with his dreams and spent a lot of time thinking and talking about Jay, transcribing conversations with close friends like Stina; during one of his many conversations with her, he discusses how it's not me he doesn't trust, it's his fucking mother who once she divorced her husband I'm sure slept around and is now involved in a relationship with a married man who is probably like the man she married to begin with only she's not married to him. Is that what Jay wants? There is no spontaneity in his behavior towards me, there is no magnanimity except in tiny little bits and pieces whenever it suits him. ("Stina's questions"; box 2, folder 1)

And, after Stina asks Islas why he continues to be with Jay, he answers, "*I don't know.* The attraction of the unattainable. The inability to accept rejection. How can he possibly reject me? Who will ever love and give to him as much as I? How can he live without knowing that *I* love him?" ("Finland 1976"; box 2, folder 1). It was on this island that Islas also began to question his past behavior with Ed Bergh. Why would he play the emotionally cold, distant partner to Ed and then the opposite role with Jay, he asked himself? Now he knew what it must have been like for Ed as the object of his tyrannical behavior. At one point, Islas even regretted leaving "Edward and my house. Why???? [only] to be consumed by passions, and jealousy the greatest of all" ("Stina's questions").

Writing and reading, in particular, helped Islas to externalize and become conscious of his behavioral patterns and allowed him to work through the trauma of his self-destructive love. He would return to this theme in his writing again and again, even exploring in his 1990 novel *Migrant Souls* how "passion had led him to believe that the Sam [Jay] he loved was real" (208). And reading provided Islas with frames of reference within which to understand himself in terms of the larger picture of human drama and tragedy. On one occasion, he writes in his journal, "Like Othello, my imagination, however, knows only those bounds circumscribed by my own sexual experience. Like him, I rant and rage and worse still, sometimes act upon what *I* have done. Such behavior can only end in stifling love" (June 30, 1978; box 9, folder 1). And Islas often filtered his need to explore the type of illusion/real duality that he felt controlled his relationship with Jay into his lectures. In a lecture on Nabokov's *Lolita,* he announces to his students, "One of the worst moments in any romantic's life is when your lover or beloved, whom you have assumed has loved you as much as you have loved him or her, tells you about the person they have felt something towards all the time they have been living with you in your fantasyland. It's a slap of reality that every romantic dreads" (Nabokov's *Lolita* lecture; box 25, folder 9).

Just before Jay put in writing the end of their relationship—"I will not play the sadist to your illusions. You must destroy them from within" (September 18, 1976; box 2, folder 7)—Islas discovered that Jay had other worlds, other realities. The inanimate *"things"* he had found in Jay's bedroom during his visit to D.C. were suddenly animated and linked to one of Jay's other "fantasylands." Jay's other world included the S&M veteran Fred Van Etta. Islas discovered that Jay liked to play the masochist to Van Etta's sadistic lashes. Jay had refused to play the masochist with him. Islas could not come to terms with the fact that his and Jay's world could exist separately from Jay's and Fred Van Etta's. Islas again felt like an outsider. Even when Islas dropped acid and had sex with Jay ("he comes after with all my fingers up his ass") to escape the painful reminders of Jay's other world (his "chapped" and "sore tits," for example), the marks on Jay's body would remind him that he was not the only one and that Jay would be returning to "Fred for the next 4 nights" (July 26, 1977; box 2, folder 1). In spite of the pain, Islas did not give up on Jay easily. He tossed and turned at night, filled with jealousy, often fantasizing about hurting Fred Van Etta: to "overwhelm and dominate him" and "to show him the *reality* of pain," as he writes in his journal on August, 25, 1976. Islas transposed his feelings of betrayal into his dreams, waking one night, for example, to recall a nightmare in which "in my next operation they will cut my legs off at the knees. . . . The city has seemed washed out, its beauty lost to me, a wasteland basking in cool bright light" (undated note; box 2, folder 1). During the day, Islas would fantasize about castrating Van Etta and "bludgeoning him to death with an ax, then whipping Jay within an inch of his life" (journal, July 1, 1977; box 2, folder 1). In another journal entry he fantasized about assuming Van Etta's role as the sadist, whipping Jay, who had told him once before, "My preference is for sex—the more and the heavier, the better" (September 4, 1976; box 2, folder 1). Finally, Islas's fantasies would find a partial release when he would seek out men who reminded him of Jay in the S&M and bathhouse scene: "You're looking for Jay in those SM bars" (journal, September 17, 1976; box 2, folder 1). On another occasion, "To the City. Dazed, bewildered, horny, anxious seeking. Weeping for Jay at the Baths. The horror of my future being one day after another like this. . . . Drive home after sexual indulgence at Boot Camp. Boring, driven, lonely" (journal, October 9, 1976; box 2, folder 1).

This is not to say that Jay completely determined the roles that Islas could play in bed. Islas could never be penetrated anally, which caused him deep insecurities and dilemmas. Sexually, he was a top, but psychologically, he acted the role of the bottom in their relationship. Even though over the years Jay grew accustomed to putting his penis, as Islas describes at one point, "between my legs, my belly down," for pleasure, Islas believed that Jay would not feel satisfied if he could not penetrate him anally. Consequently, Islas located his failure to hold Jay's sexual interest in his physical deformity. In a journal entry dated December 1, 1976, he concludes, "I have it wired up that a man is only a man if he penetrates another (anal, vaginal, the mouth seems only a fair substitute); I can't be penetrated by Jay, so I feel I'm depriving him of his manhood; this is where my mother's martyr complex enters in—suffering, renunciation, etc." (box 2, folder 1). Islas saw himself as, paradoxically, an impenetrable bottom (identifying with his mother's martyr complex his expression of "love, emotional attachment and tenderness"), making Jay's role as a top impossible to enact. So while Islas tried to enact fantasy top/bottom roles—seeking a more polymorphously perverse relation where they might have sex in either fantasy-position of domination/submission—Jay resisted, returning to Van Etta to seek a "natural" top/bottom erotic play.

FAMILY BAGGAGE

The man whom Islas felt accepted him most fully, then, was the one who most powerfully reminded him of his physical inadequacies. With Jay, however, Islas's sense of sexual undesirability wrapped around more than just his sense of being physically impenetrable. Islas also blamed their different cultures for keeping them apart. The selfless, communal part of Islas's Chicano heritage—his opening up and loving without re-serve—would always meet resistance from the exclusive world he asso-ciated with Jay's Anglo upbringing. In an undated letter to Jay titled "The first morning, pre-dawn," Islas writes, "Perhaps what defeats us is that I come from a society that taught us from the cradle to be emotionally de-pendent on other people and you come from a society that taught you to be emotionally independent of others" (box 2, folder 1). Islas identified with the part of his culture that was selfless and submissive (he associ-ated with the mother), and he identified Jay with the cold, selfish, and dominating Anglo culture.

Islas spent much of his time with his Freudian therapist, Dr. Paulsen, working out how his erotic impulses and dysfunctional relationship with Jay were linked not just to his cultural baggage but also to those closest to him—his parents, who passed down this selfish/selfless behavioral pattern. With Dr. Paulsen as his guide, Islas scrutinized his behavior, con-cluding at one point how his seeking sexual excitement in toilets and at the gym was linked to his childhood fear of not living up to his macho fa-ther's expectation of him physically. On another occasion he remarked that his estrangement from a very physical father—one whom he identi-fied strongly with the gym and playing handball at the El Paso YMCA—translated into his compulsive need to exercise in the present and "an ex-cuse for the compulsion I labor under to find him again" (journal, November 5, 1976; box 9, folder 11).

Islas used the strength he found in therapy to break with patterns of his past. He finally came out to his parents on Valentine's Day, 1977. This was a critical moment for Islas and one that he reworked into "Día de los muertos." Much to his (and his "Día" protagonist's) surprise, after com-ing out to "the Mexican *macho* cop I had feared above all other men," the father responded by saying, "Be the best goddamned homosexual there is." And after he told his mother about his love affair with Jay and his thoughts of suicide, she responded by expressing a deep sadness that he had not been able to confide in her before. In a letter to Islas written shortly after he came out to the family, his mother expresses her hope that his "suicidal feelings will disappear little by little and that your fears will also diminish with the help of your therapist," concluding, "I think you took a great step in saying—'I am a homosexual' and remember always 'God created me as me. I like myself.' Repeat this until you really believe it" (box 7, folder 11). With his parents' support, Islas experienced something like a rebirth: "I, not yet born, was still afraid of what I was. . . . I had helped my parents give birth to a son, and he was out of the closet" ("Día"). With the support of his parents—more the mother than the father—and frequent visits to Dr. Paulsen, Islas came to terms with his relationship with Jay. It was not, he realized after all, an illusion created by himself, or even the two of them. It was a profound, real love from which he could learn.

Islas's rebirth and the "shedding of an old, relentlessly clinging skin that refuses to break" gave him the strength to distance himself from Jay ("Día"). In a letter to his friend Jim Guy written a year after the breakup in April 1978, Islas remarks,

> Somehow admitting to my feelings for him *as they are* was a breakthrough for me. After last Wednesday, during his 3-hour visit, I expected to fall into a suicidal despair. I didn't. I feel it's because *for once*, I said directly to him exactly what I was feeling in the present. Have I, after all is said and done, been afraid to admit and expose to *myself* that I do indeed *love another man?* Is that what I've been fighting against? The illusions were all that parental, competitive, S/M stuff? Whether he is able to respond in kind is another matter. And, strangely enough, it doesn't matter. What does count is that I have accepted myself as a person (male) who *in fact* loves another person (male). The reality of that acceptance makes the rest real. (box 9, folder 11)

Islas had finally learned to grow from the traumatic experience—to discover and accept his own strengths and goodness by letting go of the idea of himself and his body as diseased. In a letter to Jay dated April 1978, he writes, "I will dwell and focus on [my body] and its tyrannical demands rather than on those fine qualities in me which I have never believed I possess. Until I can believe—more than that, experience it in that part of the self that is inviolable—in my worth as a person, however, physically or sexually diminished, I will not be able to lead or share the full and joyful life I want either alone or with another" (box 9, folder 11).

While Islas met and freely explored other partners after Jay, it took some time before he stopped comparing them to Jay. In journal entries after 1978, he compares, for example, Dan Dunigan's "ass and skin" to Jay's, and he writes that another partner, Steve Whitman, whom he experienced as cold and rejecting, is "JUST LIKE JAY." As time passed, Islas was able to look back on the years of trauma as a story about two men whose love would never work out because of their past (both were alienated from their fathers at an early age), their incompatible desire to role-play top or bottom, and finally, an absence of mutual desire.

"THE PLAGUE"

Just as Islas was working toward greater self-acceptance, the mainstream master narrative about HIV-AIDS sent him back to the "diseased" margins. As "gay plague" hysteria increased, shooting HIV like ammunition from a gun that targeted the "diseased" queer population generally, and as he crossed off names from his address book as one friend after another died from AIDS-related diseases, his sense of self became increasingly fragile; he curbed his sexual appetite and slowly desexualized. As the "gay plague" took those close to him, Islas increasingly turned to writing. Through writing, he transformed his S&M exploits from nights out at the Mine Shaft into the land of poetic nightmares: "Dream of Jay at a club like Boot Camp. He's naked, wearing black leather chaps and getting fucked by a stranger. He disappears. I wander about, find him in the same position. He takes my cock in his mouth" (journal, September 22, 1984; box 54, folder 7). Instead of going to bars, he wrote poems about them:

> He ties you up in the basement
> He says, he'll be right back
> He tells you he loves you
> You're still on the rack.
> Masochist, masochist.
> Upstairs you know he's got some one
> They're playing their games
> You lie there and wonder
> Where is Henry James?
> Masochist, masochist.
> Get up, get up, Isabelle

The chains are not real
Your Daddy's only human
Your waiting is his meal.
(journal, 1985; box 54, folder 7)

AIDS ravished the one Islas most loved. In 1986, Islas made up with Jay
as he became more and more ill and moved closer to death. Now, it was
the formerly "healthy" Jay who was forced to acknowledge a body
weakened by pneumonia and a chemotherapy that wreaked havoc on his
digestive system in ways that he had understood only theoretically with
Islas. As Jay became increasingly fragile, they began to reconcile their dif-
ferences and come to terms with their tumultuous past. By May of 1986,
Islas and Jay were friends again after years of bitter hostility on Islas's
part. During a visit to St. Luke's Hospital in San Francisco, Jay told Islas
that he loved him. Islas writes in his journal, "The first act is to kiss my
hand. He says everything I've always wanted to hear him say. 'I don't
hate myself anymore,' he says. 'I want to live.' When I leave, he blows me
a kiss. 'I love you,' he says" (May 26, 1986).

In spite of the reconciliation, Islas continued to find it difficult to deal
with his jealousy of Jay's partner, David Linger, who "was loyal," as Jay
told Islas, and would not abandon him as his father had (journal, May 31,
1986; box 54, folder 8). Islas had always wanted to be the one who would
not abandon Jay—the one who would be in his life like a solid rock.
Though Jay and Islas continued to work on healing, seeing Jay took its
toll, and Islas began to experience physical manifestations of stress, "my
stomach," he writes, "uncomfortable, filled with gas I am unable to
expel" (June 20, 1986; box 54, folder 8). Jay was dying; Islas received only
depressing news—"low t-cell counts, KS lesions have proliferated" (jour-
nal, June 20, 1986; box 54, folder 8). Finally, Islas realized, "I will not be
united with the person I have loved for so long. I do believe that I will be
united with my soul and that my task (very simple and not as conscious
as I am stating it) in this life and in any other I may live—or maybe for a
time in no life at all—is to come to that moment of reunion when my
body and its soul will find each other at last" (October 26, 1986; box 9,
folder 1). Days before Jay died, he told Islas over the phone how he

wanted to hold his hand but was too weak; how he did not want to say
good-bye and that he loved Islas. And in an act of reconciliation and clo-
sure Islas wrote in his journal, "You pissed me off more than anyone I've
ever known and you gave me more joy than anyone I've ever known. I'm
so grateful for it all" (November 30, 1986). After days of weeping for Jay,
Islas let go, writing in a letter to his close friend Ethel Hoffman: "When I
heard his voice on the phone—a voice I have loved deeply—all the old
rancor, bitterness, jealousy, in short, passion, disappeared and what I felt
was what I have always felt for him—just love. The temptation to sur-
render my personality to his has diminished to almost nothing; I do not
feel *I* have to go through this with him" (November 25, 1986). On De-
cember 5, 1986, at 9:30 in the morning, Jay died at the young age of thirty-
six. Islas wrote of how a "strange distance from all feeling sets in like a
fog bank."[2]

Islas made peace with Jay and then entered a period filled with an
acute sense of his own mortality: "I begin to be very sensitive to my own
physicality and sense illness everywhere" (journal, December 5, 1986;
box 54, folder 8). Islas entered into a phase of panic, silence, and hiding.
He became acutely aware of his own body as potentially "diseased," lit-
erally and metaphorically, in a prosecutorial racist and sexist mid-1980s
society. His friend Ethel had asked him to take the antibody test; he in
turn asked her to

> please not consider *me* doomed. I could not bear to be treated as if I have
> the plague by my friends or relatives. It is enough that the rest of the ar-
> rogant, ignorant world considers any and all gay people infected (and di-
> vinely so) and infectious. When that fact makes me angry—and it does—
> I remind myself that we have always been the world's most detested and
> misunderstood group of human beings and that historically, the world
> has always treated its finest people with disdain and cruelty, whatever
> their sexuality. But I have always wondered what threat fragile fairies
> over the centuries have posed for the Great Pyramids of Straightdom.
> What an ineffably sad mystery! (November 25, 1986)

AIDS became the spotlight that exposed subjects like Islas as "diseased"
and that, as Islas wrote, expressed profound social fears and anxieties

through racism, patriotism, and homophobia. For Islas and others, then, the "gay plague" became yet another system of surveillance that controlled the pleasure of queer bodies.

Islas's sense of being under surveillance as a "diseased" body in the 1980s was not entirely new. Years earlier, in a prophetic letter he wrote to "mom, dad, Louie, Mario," he describes how

> people like us cannot be happy in the world because the world is against us from the very beginning. Not because of any intrinsic desire on our part to be unhappy, but because the world is simply repelled by the idea of two people of the same sex (especially two men) expressing their love for each other. It will take a long, long time to change the world's attitude and it certainly won't happen in my life time. I despair. (February 12, 1978; box 53, folder 3)

Islas had always been attuned to the hypocrisy of a society that would criminalize his monogamous relationships while embracing a figure like his father—a bully and an adulterer (see journal entry, February 12, 1978; box 53, folder 3). Islas always felt deformed, not just because of his limp and colostomy bag (his character Miguelito exclaims at one point how he "saw it as a cruel emblem of what separated me from other people"), but also because of how he was imagined by a homophobic straight society to be a diseased criminal. The AIDS era only exacerbated Islas's sense of the mainstream forcing him to be the perverse negative of heterosexuality and also the dirty, impure negative of whiteness.[3]

FOUR

Death and Rebirth

Arturo Islas spent his life challenging the many boundaries that threat-ened to enclose him within restrictive roles—intellectual, filial, sexual, and racial. He also spent a lifetime struggling to come to terms with a bod-ily existence compromised by illness. That Islas was preoccupied with mortality is no surprise. His childhood—which was imbued with life/death dualistic Catholic doctrine as well as a small dose of Seventh Day Adventist apocalyptic drama—reminded him that physical existence was temporary and would ultimately come to an end. Family stories often gravitated around death. His awareness of mortality deepened when he himself almost died from polio. Two decades later, death would return to visit a thirty-year-old Islas when an ulcerated colon led to a radical colostomy that saved his life but left him feeling like half-a-man. His de-cided limp, along with the plastic appliance attached to the gut—the "stinky rose" protruding from his stomach—left Islas feeling monstrously deformed. He turned to self-destructive abuse of alcohol and drugs in the mid-1970s. After a decade of substance abuse, Islas realized that he needed to take charge of his life and not escape into the never-never land of drugs and alcohol. Ironically, it was during this period, as Islas was beginning to shed bad habits and regain a sense of being physically and emotionally healthy, that he tested positive for HIV.

POLIO

Even before he contracted polio, Arturo Islas immersed himself in the world of literature and history—a world to which he could escape without censure from his father. After his bout with polio, his self-image as a fragile body with limited kinetic movement amplified ten-fold. As an adult, Islas reflected that his insatiable appetite for consuming healthy bodies of knowledge was a way to escape an overwhelming sense of inhabiting an unhealthy body: "I've always been a sickly person. I've always had one illness after another and I had polio when I was eight years old. That really changed my life in some way because my left leg was paralyzed so I had this limp. I could not keep up physically with the other kids, so I became very studious" (Burciaga interview, November 28, 1990; box 2, folder 1).

Of course, escaping into a corpus of knowledge was Islas's only option for escaping a postpolio deformed body and the father he blamed for this bringing on this condition. He was, after all, a young boy still completely dependent on his father and mother. And it was Arturo Sr. who held, as young Islas believed, the strings that determined his fate physically. In the fall of 1946, an eight-year-old Islas woke from a nap one afternoon complaining of a backache, inexplicable fatigue, and vision that was blurring at the edges. Too young to know about the polio virus, Islas believed that death had arrived for him: God had finally come to judge if he was a saint or a sinner. His mother, Jovita, suspected that something was medically wrong and urged Arturo Sr. to take the young Islas to the doctor. But the father was convinced that Islas was merely acting like he was sick—not to get out of going to school, but to spend the day with his mother. Arturo Islas Sr. expressly forbade Jovita to take Islas to the doctor. The following day, Islas had a difficult time commanding his legs to move; he could barely get out of bed and dress for school. As per the father's orders, Islas went to school. Jovita, however, stepped from her dutiful role as the passive wife and took charge as the mother of her son. She called Islas at school and told him to take the bus downtown to visit their family doctor. She would meet him there after work. Islas made it on to the bus, but by the time it stopped near their family doctor's office, he was too weak to walk; a passenger had to carry him off the bus and to the office. Jovita met young Islas at the doctor's and while they waited their turn, both felt waves of guilt and betrayal toward the father as well as an overwhelming sense of imminent death. To the doctor, Islas's symptoms immediately suggested polio—a virus that had taken many young lives in this pre-vaccine era. The doctor gave him pain medications and recommended that he be withdrawn from school immediately and sent to a sanitarium. Several days later, blood test results confirmed that Islas had contracted the virus. Soon after, he was removed from school and sent away to a nearby state sanitarium to convalesce and to prevent the spread of the virus to his classmates and others.

Islas's brush with death resulted in that which his father most feared: the event became a centrifugal act, spinning the father further away from a mother/son planetary core. Islas and the mother harbored not just a deep sense of anger toward the father—she believed that if Islas had been diagnosed earlier he would not have developed the limp—but also a sense of guilt that they had betrayed the will of the father. In fact, the polio virus acts according to its own rhythms, so even if Islas had been treated earlier—in the hospital the first day of its inception, for example—the virus would have followed its course. Holding Arturo Sr. accountable for the limp helped the mother and son to deal with these emotions of guilt and betrayal.

Within the white-washed, sanitized, and regulated sanitarium, Islas cultivated a deep sense of guilt for having acted against the father. He felt he was being punished for transgressing the law. He had been exiled and, as a consequence, his deepening engagement with the world of books and learning at school would be delayed. However, his illness and distance from home life also gave Islas a sense of empowerment. Suffering physically and coming close to death opened Islas's eyes to the power of resisting and challenging the patriarchal master. Once Islas returned from the sanitarium, he was less willing to submit to his father's threats of punishment. And, he was less willing to please the father to gain his attention and favor. His resistance would have to be subtle to avoid his father's wrath. It would take shape in his immersion in the life of the mind. Knowledge would function not only as a means of escaping his deformed body, but also as a form of resistance to a world governed by laws, expectations (physical), and gaze of the father. After school and on weekends, Islas would spend his time in his room working on extra homework assignments and reading books he would regularly borrow from the library; when family dramas unfolded, he would retreat to his favorite spot under a cherry tree in the backyard to read for hours at a time. Through his reading and studying, young Islas learned to live more freely within the otherwise restrictive confines of a patriarchally circumscribed household and within a physically limited body.

After Islas finished elementary school and junior high, he realized his childhood dream of entering El Paso High—the school his parents attended and the public school with the best academic curriculum. Islas put more and more distance between himself and his home life, spending more and more time at school participating in extracurricular activities like playing in the marching band and the orchestra. And, after a surgery that minimized his limp by slowing the growth of his healthy right leg, he began to test more and more the limits of his body: he became famous on the high school campus for his agile and daring dance movements at social functions. His pugnacious spirit was coming to the fore—something he inherited from his father—but he was also escaping the complex array of emotions generated from his less-than-whole self-image. High school, then, was the site where Islas was first able to determine his everyday activities away from his dysfunctional family environment and also where he could use his smarts, good looks, and overachiever spirit to mask his deeply felt bodily insecurity.

WRITING THE BODY

In high school, Islas harbored dreams of becoming a doctor—specifically a neurosurgeon. He had experienced firsthand the miracle of science and medicine that had brought him back from the edge of death as a child and that, in a surgical operation to his right leg, had lessened dramatically his postpolio limp. As a doctor, Islas would not only understand the body as a biological entity governed by systematic rules and regulations, but also help others overcome their bodily limitations. So, in high school Islas immersed himself in science, excelling especially at biology and physics. He learned the basics of science and also how to read and analyze his own body. Studying science was a way for him to better understand—and externalize—his own physical disability. There were others worse off and, as far as Islas was concerned, there was much work that still needed to be done in the medical field so that diseases like polio would be eradicated.

As Islas moved through high school, however, he came to feel that science lacked a human element. Islas craved the knowledge offered by science, but also thirsted for metaphysical knowledge. By his senior year in high school, he was somewhat divided between the idea of pursuing a scientific course of study or one that would open doors to the imagination and an understanding of being in the world. So, though he focused more on science—even winning a science scholarship for college—he read history, philosophy, and literature voraciously.

During his first year at Stanford in 1956–57, his desire to become a medical doctor underwent a permutation. By the end of his first year, the world of literature and writing pointed to a more attractive way for him to access the complexity of the human condition. In a journal entry that looks back at this transitional period, Islas writes of his realization that literature can also "bolster the immune system" (February 20, 1987). Instead of preparing for a life of incising the flesh, he would pursue a course of study wherein he would learn to analyze the body with the razor-sharp edge of his mind. By his junior year, Islas had completely made the shift from the sciences to the humanities, declaring himself an

English major with a minor in French. Fully immersed in the study of literature, Islas found himself particularly drawn to those writers who suffered from some form of physical deformity or alienation. He identified strongly with Heathcliff's sense of estrangement and alienation in *Wuthering Heights;* he also grew to feel a lifelong affinity for the writer Henry James, with whom Islas strongly identified because he also "felt estranged as a child [and equally] incompetent" (Carson MuCullers lecture; box 25, folder 7). And Islas was moved by and deeply related to other outcast writers whose impaired sense of self informed their fictions. Writers that he thought of deeply and often were Carson McCullers, who had suffered from pneumonia and undiagnosed rheumatic fever as a teenager; Flannery O'Connor, who had struggled with lupus; Hart Crane, who had been "frail and unhealthy" but who had envisioned strong, new poetic architectures; and Walt Whitman, who had found moments of relief in writing from his "attacks of depression."

As an upperclassman at Stanford, Islas was a serious student, spending long hours studying literature and writing scholarly essays and narrative fiction; he was especially interested in exploring life from the vantage point of the physically disfigured and through the eyes of the weak and powerless. (Later, as a professor at Stanford, his interest in the imperfect author would become the focus of many lectures on American literature; see chapter 5.) It was in and through literature—and its various intersections with history and philosophy—that Islas found ways to understand the trauma of his childhood, which had been filled with a sense of physical and psychological powerlessness. In and through literature, Islas felt he could transform his sense of being a diseased outsider into a deeper insight into "things and people" (Carson McCullers lecture).

Islas worked diligently to sharpen his craft as a writer and a thinker. He knew by the end of his senior year that this would be the place for him to explore the complex terrain of human emotion. From the point of view of the powerless and estranged subjects that inhabit different fictional worlds, he would understand himself and others better. Islas's BA with honors in English and strong faculty support gained him entrance to the PhD program, where he could continue with his reading, thinking, and writing at a more in-depth level. By the time he finished his PhD in English and began teaching as a professor in the Stanford English department, he had boxes filled with scholarly essays on authors that had struggled with variously ailed bodies from John Milton to Walt Whitman, from Jorge Luis Borges to Henry James; he also had boxes filled with carefully crafted autobiographical short stories and poems that explored his own relationship to a deformed body.

As Islas began his teaching career at Stanford in the early 1970s, he began to move away from writing scholarly essays, turning more and more to the writing of narrative fiction and poetry. Though he continued to write essays, he found that narrative fiction and poetry provided the space he needed to externalize and understand better his past and present life, which gravitated around traumas of the body. In a first draft of his "Día de los muertos," Islas expands his childhood encounter with polio. Here he fleshes out for the first time an autobiographically informed character-as-self, Miguelito, to showcase the complex perspective of an eight-year-old deeply hurt by his father's rejection: "He's only being a brat [who] was pretending to be sick so that he wouldn't have to go to school" ("Día"; box 5, folder 4). In the world of narrative fiction, especially in the longer form that the novel afforded, Islas could experience a tremendous amount of freedom to explore the human psyche. He could also use fiction to redesign his world as a reinvented eight-year-old, investing his character with the experience and wisdom of an adult looking back and analyzing retrospectively. For example, he has his character interpret the polio episode as the father character's attempt to break into the "intricately woven web of feeling" between son and mother. And in a further fictionalized transformation, Islas's narrator-protagonist sees his father in a light that allows him to understand his actions and also to articulate the gulf of emotion that separates father from son:

> If later in that year and throughout his life he made excuses to himself and others for his behavior towards his oldest child, Miguel Grande never forgave himself. Nor could he bring himself to express his regret to Miguel Chico. It pained him to see his son walk, and he invented ways to make a man of him. One of his devices had been to ask Miguelito's school friends to engage him in fistfights so that he might learn to defend himself. Another was to enroll him in advanced swimming classes at the YMCA with

private instructions to the teacher to be twice as hard on him as on the other boys his age. All of his attempts failed because Juanita found out about them and protected her son even more vigilantly. Miguel Chico ignored his body and became a scholar.

With "Día de los muertos," Islas came into a sense of the power of writing autobiographically informed fiction to refigure and remember the dis-membered family unit of his past. Islas could relive and redesign those broken emotions as they intertwined with his deformed body and with his conflictive feelings toward his father.

Increasingly, Islas turned to creative writing as a way to explore his insecurities and self-mutilatory impulses, which stemmed from indirect and direct social pressures to be physically perfect. In his everyday behavior and activity, Islas masked his deep insecurities and depressions. During the day, in front of his students and colleagues, he performed fulfillment, happiness, and health. At night, as a writer, he struggled to come to terms with a warped self-image that pictured him as ugly, diseased, and deformed. The writing helped him fight his demons; it also made him more conscious of the "real" feelings that lay underneath an "illusory" Islas. Behind the mask of success as one of Stanford's first Chicano professors in the humanities, he was in fact terribly unhappy. At one point, he began to think he might be manic depressive because of the intensity of his childhood and his sense of himself as a sensitive, creative individual. He was faced with a paradox. The writing would help him explore and work out emotional tensions and contradictions within; but it would also serve as an escape from the daily experience of insecurities that led him simultaneously to radiate success and drown himself in drugs and alcohol.

LIFE WITH THE "SCAT BAG"

There was more to Islas's creative writing than an untangling of complex emotions stemming from his past and present familial and personal relationships. He also explored, in narrative fiction such as "Día de los muertos" and his early poems, the trauma of surviving a colostomy in 1969 that left him with an even more radically imperfect self-image. The colostomy radically altered his everyday life: he had to learn to incorporate the presence of a colostomy bag at his side, a constant reminder of his body's physical limitations.

Islas had suffered from stomach pain and long stretches of severe diarrhea some years before, waking up one morning in 1962 with searing abdominal pain. Doubled over at the edge of his bed, he was reminded of the time sixteen years earlier when he contracted polio. The symptoms were different, but the excruciating pain was the same; his body seemed to be looping back to repeat a like narrative. He checked himself into the Stanford Medical Health Center immediately. He was diagnosed not with polio, but with chronic ulcerative colitis. The doctors sent him home with a prescription of the antibiotic ampicillin. As the days passed, the pain subsided, and Islas considered the problem cured. As the years passed, however, his stomach would fire up with sudden attacks of abdominal pain with increasing frequency. It became more and more difficult for him to work. During this period, he would check in to the Stanford Medical Health Center, go on antibiotics, experience temporary relief, and then return to his research, his writing, and his life. At one point during the mid-1960s, when Islas was taking some time off from the PhD program to gather up some "real world" experience (he worked a variety of different jobs, including one as a language instructor at the Menlo Park veterans hospital), he realized that his stomach was not getting any better. Concerned that he would not be able to afford a medical bill if anything were to happen, he returned to Stanford, where he would be covered by medical insurance.

Islas's instincts were right. The diarrhea and abdominal pains sharpened, and his visits to the hospital to repair his body were longer and more protracted. Of course, Islas was sexually active during this period, so he was anxious that perhaps the doctors had misdiagnosed his symptoms and that his ailments were STD related. He checked himself in on one occasion because he noticed some discharge from his penis and the appearance of genital warts. Perhaps, he thought, his body was responding to an STD. However, after a series of visits between February and

March 1969, Stanford Medical sent him home diagnosed with having contracted an E coli bacterial infection. They upped the dosage of ampicillin, adding to it a heavy dose of another antibiotic. This time, however, Islas did not recuperate, as he had before. The drugs only seemed to aggravate the pain in his stomach. By the beginning of April 1969, the pain was so severe that Islas could barely function in his everyday activities; he certainly could not concentrate on his dissertation. He checked in to the Stanford Medical yet again, this time with a high fever and an unstoppable flow of diarrhea. After a couple of days of bed rest and another round of antibiotics, the doctors sent Islas back home. A week later, Islas still did not feel well, so he checked in with his doctor for more testing. He was told that the E coli infection had cleared, but that he had another case of chronic ulcerative colitis. He went on prednisone to slow down the abdominal inflammation that appeared to be exacerbating the colitis. In the weeks that followed, the drugs did not appear to be working. He continued to have severe diarrhea and a slight fever. In May 1969 Islas was admitted to the hospital. This time, however, he was on the brink of death. Dr. John Kieraldo did emergency surgery, performing a resection of the diseased intestine and surgical formation of an artificial anus. The surgery saved Islas's life, but it would also radically alter both his body and his sense of self. In "American Dream and Fantasies," he recreates the event:

> As the surgeon and anesthetist lifted me gently out of the gurney and onto the hard cold table, each on either side of me spoke quietly about what they were going to do. I was impressed by their voices, tender and kind. I was even more impressed by the way they were touching me, as if I were a person in pain, a rare ability in most nurses and doctors. I thought in those seconds that if these were the last human voices I heard, that would be fine with me, and I longed to be unconscious and escape from the drugged and disembodied state of twilight I had lived in for weeks. (box 12, folder 3)

Once he recovered from the surgeries, Islas embarked on a new struggle: to incorporate and normalize the presence of a plastic tube sticking from his gut (his "stinky-rose," as he called it) and that plugged into the receptacle ("shit bag" or "scat bag") that hung from his side.

Through writing, Islas likely circumvented what might have led to a postoperative psychological neurosis, transforming his despair into narrative fiction and poetry. Through the eyes of an array of different protagonists and poet-narrators, Islas humanized this traumatic and deeply alienating experience. For Islas, discomfort and suffering once again became an opportunity to excavate, explore, learn, and empower himself. This does not negate the suffering he experienced. The fiction carries with it the intense sense of pain he felt as he awoke, for example, on a hospital gurney with tubes protruding from virtually every opening of his body as well as the agonizing sense that his life would be "forever a slave to plastic appliances" ("American Dreams").

The medical crisis could not have come at a worse time for Islas. He was just beginning to confidently explore physicality with other male bodies, experiencing the very different pleasures of being a top (penetrator) and being a bottom (penetrated), just learning of his generally greater pleasure as a bottom. The site from which he had begun to derive so much sensuous pleasure—the anus—would become for Islas a "phantom rectum," akin to a phantom limb.

The surgeries and the resulting physical deformation affected more than his sexual pleasure, however. Islas was exquisitely conscious that the queer rectum was the bodily site most abhorred by a homophobic society as dirty, perverse, abnormal. He characterized the colostomy as a literalization of the heterosexist fantasy: to remove the rectum as a site of pleasure and erase a form of sexuality traditionally coded as *contra natura*. A body without a rectum, a body forever dependent on a "shit bag" was a literal manifestation of what Islas already felt as a gay man in a world that taught him to imagine his body as unsanitary and his rectum the ultimate source of shame. Islas turned to writing to explore the literal and metaphoric inhabiting of a mutilated body that oozed shit. His poem "Scat Bag" (box 9, folder 2) begins:

> Fragrant, red mouth at my side
> surrounded, encased in plastic
> You remind me relentlessly of my mortality
> What shall I do with this constant ooze?"

Islas used poetry writing to come to terms with becoming the shit that society had already labeled him. The poem speaks to his feeling forced to seek intimacy in textual and not bodily forms: "the lover who walks away / After telling you it did not work." The poem ends with images of the freedom of flying in gas-filled balloons, which he deflates in the stanza's final lines:

> Tugged at the belly towards the ceiling.
> We don't belong there. We are grounded.
> *That's* illusion. It amuses and that's why
> I need it. Any distraction. Anything
> Except the fear of dying
> Fetid human bag packaged for the twentieth century
> Our dark age has come to this. These bags will
> Sell for a dime. Want to give a friend a bag
> Of shit? Plastic naturalism.

Islas's ulcerative colitis did not lead him to romantic wanderings in search of a cure. Rather, like the gas balloon he described in "Scat Bag," Islas yearned to escape the reality of his condition but could not fly.

After his surgeries, Islas became completely dependent on Stanford; as long as he stayed employed with Stanford, he would have the health insurance he needed to cover the expensive supplies for his "scat bag" and the antibiotics needed to kill off infections. He knew that he would have to secure a more permanent professional relationship with Stanford, not just to gain a living, but to secure medical benefits. Islas asked friend and mentor Wallace Stegner for help. In a letter, Stegner advised him to request an extension on the dissertation, which he had still not finished, and to talk to the department chair, Ian Watt, about extending his one-year appointment as an instructor (July 17, 1970; box 39, folder 23). As they had when Islas first became ill as a graduate student, Watt and Stegner took the steps necessary for Islas to remain at Stanford and finish his work. He was granted extensions and given employment as an adjunct lecturer. He finished his dissertation. He was hired into a tenure-track position. His umbilical cord to the institution remained fully intact. During Islas's recovery and reinhabiting of a new body, Stanford became a surrogate parent that provided him with sympathy and care.[1] It also became his crutch.

During the 1970s Islas struggled to live with his new plastic body parts and with his new dependency on Stanford. He began to feel comfortable sleeping on his left side, which would keep him from waking up with a burst plastic bag and feces-stained sheets. Even changing the bag became routine. He writes matter-of-factly in his journal: "Change appliance. Meet Jay. Rent car" (July 17, 1976; box 2, folder 1). However, living as a half-plastic/half-organic body in the world took its toll on Islas, both psychologically and physically. He had to spend extended periods of time convalescing at the Stanford Medical Center during this period, and he felt angry and frustrated that his body had shackled him—to his scat bag, and also to Stanford. With the exception of his living with his parents for a year in El Paso in 1987–88, he rarely spent more than a month or two away from Stanford. He felt more than ever an object under constant surveillance: he was under the watchful eye of the department—especially during sick leaves—and had to check regularly with the medical center. The very fact that he imagined his body a "plastic naturalism" meant that he could never erase his deep sense of himself as deformed and under the constant watch of an institutional gaze. He needed Stanford, but his dependency was a constant reminder of his status as a sick body. He could not escape his sense of disfigurement even in his dreams, writing in his journal "that my stoma has fallen out and is all mixed up with organs, mushrooms and fettuccini" (December 1978; box 53, folder 3).

And, of course, his scat bag was a constant reminder of his sexual limitations. After a Friday night out in San Francisco, Islas writes in his journal, "I let myself run the gamut of sexual jealousy on this one. No asshole! No asshole!" (October 6, 1978; box 53, folder 3). Islas spent a lifetime wrestling with his deep insecurities about not being a "whole" man and his inability to perform the role of the penetrable bottom to lovers like Jay Spears. Islas's narrator in "Día de los muertos" laments at one point, "I saw it as a cruel emblem of what separated me from other people" (box 12, folder 1).

For a while, Islas turned to S&M role-playing to work through deep feelings about bodily mutilation. When he role-played the masochist, the pain to which he was subjected helped to externalize his deep psychic pain. Through the physical pain of an S&M session Islas could overcome (if only temporarily) thoughts of an impure versus pure body. The feelings of shame and anger toward the plastic tube that projected from his body and that marked his physical difference would at least momentarily be displaced in acts of S&M. By role-playing an exaggerated version of what he already felt himself to be—an object of shame—he worked through psychological barriers. The pain and creative role-playing in S&M, he felt, helped him to come to terms with an object that otherwise nagged at him like an incurable low-grade infection.

DRINK

S&M, creative fiction, and poetry all functioned as venues for Islas to cope with and work through the psychological conflicts that gravitated around his feelings of bodily disease. There was, however, another, less creative antidote. During the 1970s, alcohol binges became more and more common as a way for Islas to try to wash away his feelings of deep bodily shame and his sense of failure as a lover to Jay Spears.

This was a period of tremendous psychological turmoil for Islas. It was a time when he was learning not only to inhabit a newly constrained body, but also when he was testing the limits of his sexual freedom as a gay Chicano throwing off the shackles of his rigid Catholic upbringing. It was a time when he sought novel, polymorphous experiences with multiple partners; but he also wanted a committed relationship with one man, Jay Spears. It was the time when he suffered most from the push-pull tug of Jay's alternations of acceptance and rejection. To escape from this maelstrom of conflictive emotion, he turned to alcohol. He would gulp all the emotion down "with scotch and soda," as he fictionalizes in *Migrant Souls* (192). Whether scotch and soda or gin and tonic (his favorite), he drank heavily and usually into the late hours of the night to bring calm to his balled-up frustration, anger, and pain, all of which stemmed from his acute sense of being physically deformed and unwanted: "at least three half gallons of each for future battle and skirmishes," his fictionalized self, Miguelito, declares in his short story "The Dead."

Alcohol became a way for Islas to hide from his feelings of shame and despair; it also functioned as a daily ritual by which he could maintain the illusion of controlling his feelings; just as he had control over the process of mixing his scotch and soda over ice, so he could pretend control over his emotions. As he became more and more an expert at this ritual, he became more and more dependent on alcohol, and he sank deeper and deeper into a self-destructive pattern. By the end of the 1970s, Islas had to drink just to feel like he could get through the day. A typical journal entry from this period reads: "Tues: 3 Scotches, 1 beer, 1 snort." He was aware that his drinking was a problem—often writing in his journal about his breaking vows "to stop drinking once and for all" (February 7, 1978; box 53, folder 3). He was also intent on keeping other people from knowing about it. His controlling of a public self-image of the good boy also worked to feed his delusion of being in control. Without fully realizing it at the time, Islas became a high-functioning alcoholic who hid his inner chaos beneath a surface of grace and control. He rarely let alcohol get in the way of his work and did not allow it to alter his polished behavior at social gatherings. Most of his close friends had no idea that he was an alcoholic, and there was nothing in his professional life that indicated that Islas had a problem. He received promotions and was working hard on a promising novel.

As Islas consumed more and more alcohol, his body steadily built up tolerance. But he could not always be under the influence of alcohol; as the numbing wore off, thoughts of suicide and reminders of his physical deformity, shame, guilt, and anger toward his body, Jay Spears, his family, and the world would surface again. Rather than deal with the problems directly and one by one, he would use these feelings to nourish his justifications for giving into another binge that would incapacitate him for days. He also used the justification that he was a writer. Writers like Carson McCullers, F. Scott Fitzgerald, and William Faulkner, he reasoned, turned to alcohol and to writing as ways to externalize and so exorcise their suffering.

It was not until the early 1980s that Islas finally decided that he needed to take active steps to change course. His earlier ability to function in his everyday life was diminishing. He would wake late after typing all night to read over pages he thought he filled with creative excellence, only to realize they were complete nonsense. And his strategy of plotting out and carefully scripting lectures no longer worked effectively. He found himself inarticulate with students during discussions; finally, he no longer had the energy needed to perform his lectures and so would end them early or cancel them altogether. Bouts of deep depression returned, no matter how much he drank. His early morning dry heaves increased in frequency and force.[2] He was more down than up and feared he might lose his job, friends, and his mind and body, so he decided to systematically wean himself from what he identified as his "addictions": cocaine and alcohol. The results were immediate. Beginning in the fall of 1983, he writes in his journal of periods when he feels for the first time that his life is "less cluttered" and has more "more energy" (September 14, 1983; box 54, folder 6). Islas struggled to stay sober in the months and years that followed. At first, any sign of rejection or feeling of depression would send him back to the bottle—and back to cocaine. After a couple of months of sobriety, he would break down and drink again, reflecting in his journal how it "definitely affects me *negatively*." "Stop it! Please," he writes (April 30, 1984; box 54, folder 7).

The less alcohol—and drugs like cocaine—he consumed, the more he could see his dependency with clarity and the more he was resolved to stop. However, after years of struggling on his own, he realized that he would need professional help. He confided in colleague and poet Kenneth Fields at Stanford (who was at the time a recovering alcoholic), who recommended a good Alcoholics Anonymous clinic in the nearby city of San Jose. It was close enough to be convenient, yet far enough away from the Stanford campus for Islas to maintain his anonymity. So, on January 28, 1986, Islas checked in to this AA clinic. At the first meeting he admitted for the first time in public that he was an abuser of alcohol and drugs who had tried to cure himself but failed. This was a period of rebirth for Islas: he began his twelve-step recovery program with AA; he returned to the church for the first time since his rejection as a little boy; and he began to practice meditation and to study Buddhism.

With the help of Eastern philosophy and meditation, along with the church and AA, Islas slowly weaned himself of his substance abuse. He writes of how the fourth step involves "a rigorous self-examination about past misdeeds while under the influence," and that led him to interrogate his own "selfish poses and demands, willful blindness and self-centered wishes" (undated note; box 3, folder 1). To heal fully, Islas knew that he would not only have to face his problems, but also have to learn lasting strategies for fighting—and not escaping—his demons. He learned, for example, to accept his own responsibility for playing the role of the martyr/victim. He writes of his realization that "alcohol has been my substitute" and that he had used equations such as "Alcohol = abusive lover = Jay! = obsession = Death = Catholic Romantic Love" to justify his alcoholism (journal, January 30, 1986; box 54, folder 8). By the time Islas passed into his sixth step of recovery, he writes in his journal how "fear, anxiety, anger, envy, paranoia, self-pity, the inferiority/superiority complex" are the "ancient forces" that he must learn to overcome (April 15, 1987; box 2, folder 1). As such, Islas learned to fight his demons and acknowledge his own complicit role in his destructive behavior.

On January 28, 1987, he writes in his journal how he is able to see, taste, and feel the world more sharply and with a greater spiritual awareness. He had been sober for a full year and felt as if reborn. He knew, however, that while he had learned strategies for understanding himself and his demons better, the struggle was not over. On March 23, 1987, he writes in his journal, "I am a living nerve end w/ a great desire to deaden this vulnerability w/ alcohol." During this period, Islas's struggle was during both waking and sleeping hours; he often wrote of waking from nightmares about alcohol. Just before his first-year anniversary celebrating his sobriety, he wrote in his journal how in a dream "I'm drinking champagne out of a table spoon, am roaring drunk, alternately contentious, angry at others, disgusted with myself. Still, I keep ladling it in. All vaguely connected to Jay. My unresolved anger towards him has become a habit. Time to be rid of it!" (January 6, 1987; box 2, folder 1). Later, he records dreaming that "I casually throw away my sobriety and drink a beer. So real, I awaken believing it happened" (February 21, 1987; box 2, folder 1). Ultimately, Islas used the twelve-step program, Christianity, his meditation, and Eastern philosophy as guides to a better life. In a letter to friend Gloria Velásquez-Treviño, he writes, "Suffering is not necessarily a requirement. In fact, joy can be a greater source of artistic inspiration than grief" (letter, box 43, folder 18). He describes how he has come to terms with his desperate desire to be loved and to find love outside of himself, discovering instead, he writes, "that it is inside of me and that it's my job to put it out there, it was like a revelation. It made me stop being so needy of others' approval *and* disapproval (they are two sides of the same coin)" (box 43, folder 18).

Giving up alcohol meant giving up a self-image as a writer who relied on alcohol to externalize pain. Islas cured himself of his alcohol and drug addictions and began to turn a corner in terms of his health and clarity of mind. Tragically, just as Islas had mastered his self-destructive substance abuse, he tested positive for HIV. This did not send him into another psychological tailspin, however. He continued to use meditation, and spiritual faith, and his AA group meetings as strategies to strengthen himself bodily and spiritually to fight this next battle.

HUMAN IMMUNODEFICIENCY VIRUS

Long before January 14, 1988, when Islas received the results that he had tested positive for HIV, he had been living in a world that reminded him constantly of the fragility of his life. Since 1981, when scientists first identified what was called the "gay cancer" and first named GRID (Gay Related Immuno Deficiency), Islas's awareness of mortality and his sense of inhabiting a disfigured body had been intensifying. He belonged to the community the media had identified as the progenitor of the "gay plague." During this period, Islas was surrounded by reminders of death: many of his close friends and ex-partners showed symptoms of "GRID," swiftly deteriorating physically and then dying from a related illness. In many of his journal entries, Islas began to note when his friends came down with the "plague" and when they died. This began as early as September 6, 1983, when he wrote of one such friend, Bill, who had died of what was finally called "AIDS"; entries proliferated as friends were diagnosed, fell ill, and died.

This only heightened Islas's own sense of a deformed body and his already acute sense of his own mortality. He began to withdraw from ex-

perimental sex play and refrained from cruising the streets for anony-
mous sex. This was not just because of HIV, but because of the increased
homophobia across America and especially in San Francisco's tradition-
ally safe gay/lesbian enclaves like South of Market and the Castro. By
1983 homophobic violence had amplified dramatically in San Francisco,
sparked by a press that identified the gay plague as having "infected"
heterosexual couples. Many gays and lesbians used this as an opportu-
nity to galvanize and fight homophobia and heterosexual panic. Islas re-
sponded differently, self-protectively withdrawing from social contact
and distancing himself from loved ones. He kept his new partner, Jim
Guy, at arm's length, fearing losing him (Guy was diagnosed HIV-
positive). For Islas, it was as if the clock had been turned back to the mid-
1950s, when he was also deathly afraid of loving other men, albeit for dif-
ferent reasons. Living in a climate filled with, as he writes in his journal,
"fear and hysteria over AIDS and death" sickened and angered Islas
(July 22, 1983; box 2, folder 1). In March 1986, Islas received news that the
love of his life, Jay Spears, had contracted HIV and was struggling to
overcome the "brain seizures and psychotic moments" of full-blown
AIDS (journal, March 13, 1986; box 2, folder 1). The 1980s was unfolding
as an apocalyptic decade for Islas, taking away much of the sexual and
psychological freedoms he had struggled so long to attain.

Living in a culture that reminded him of death at every turn, it is
hardly surprising that Islas began to obsess over his health and his body.
After Spears's death in December 1986, especially, he would monitor
every new line and texture that appeared on his skin, mouth, tongue,
arms, hands, and groin. Each morning he would wake up to read, reread,
then read again his body as if it were a literary text, looking for corporeal
inscriptions that might anticipate an abrupt shift in the uncertain narra-
tive of his life. In a journal entry dated March 2, 1987, he remarks,
"Canker sores in my mouth; one under the right upper lip; one on the
uvula; little one on the roof of my mouth" (box 2, folder 1). He had been
through physical difficulties before, of course, but this was different—a
time of intense self-monitoring and surveillance, a time when every dot,
blemish, and sore was recorded in detail. The time and duration of a cold
sore, a bruise, or a minor skin irritation all became potential signs of

"unhealthiness" that might indicate the "truth" of his body's internal transformations, signs that would otherwise be invisible to the naked eye and that spoke, he writes, of "a larger condition" (March 2, 1987; box 2, folder 1). Increasingly, every blemish, from a flea bite to a canker sore, became charged with deadly significance. Islas lived in a constant state of fear and mental imbalance; he constantly slipped into deliberations over past sexual encounters and the possibility of having been exposed to HIV.

His everyday deliberations, coupled with his obsessive readings of his body's textures, led him to a new set of dead-ends. He felt he could no longer trust his memory of his pre–gay plague body's adventures, and he began to doubt his detailed readings of his current body, treating his body as if it were an "unreliable narrator" that could no longer speak with reliable authority. After discovering an unfamiliar spot on his nose, Islas writes how he is no longer sure how to read the text of his body: it could either be a blemish resulting "from stress" or a first sign of "AIDS eczema" (October 12, 1987; box 2, folder 1). And, after reading two blood blisters that appeared on his inner lower lip one morning, he immediately jumps to the conclusion, "my days are numbered" (October 19, 1987; box 2, folder 1). He continues, "For over 24 hours I give myself the *terrors*. The *day* turns crimson with anxiety" (October 19, 1987). The blisters disappear, and his interpretation of his body's texture shifts once again. His body becomes an ever-mutating story with an unreliable narrator that determines more and more an everyday life filled with self-doubt and fear. In his journal on November 14, 1987, he writes powerfully, "I pray that the terror and quiet dread be taken away."

As much as he feared and mistrusted his own readings, he was loath to seek out the reading of a medical doctor. Rather, as if attached to the daily suspense, he persisted in reading his own body's textures. This was partly a survival mechanism: maintaining a state of uncertainty seemed a better option than knowing for sure that he had HIV. It was also partly a response to the social climate: social denigration and exile were promised to anyone tainted by the merest hint of HIV. Islas writes of breaking out in a cold sweat as he watched "a bracing, horrifying program on AIDS" on *Nightline* during a visit with his friend Ethel Hoffman in Albuquerque, New Mexico. After the program was over, with Ethel sitting at his side, Islas worried that she would reevaluate their friendship, concluding his journal entry with: "I wish I hadn't seen it" (January 9, 1987). As far as Islas was concerned, to expose himself to a medical examination would be akin to making his body visible as "perverse" and "diseased," regardless of his HIV status; such exposure, he felt certain, would certify his own social death.[3]

By September 1987, Islas's body was telling him a disturbingly reliable story. No longer able to deny his body's consistent narrative texturing of HIV symptoms, a desperate Islas made an appointment with Dr. Babb at the Palo Alto Medical Center for a general checkup. He harbored the hope that a medical exam might tell him a more positive story than the one that was unraveling before his eyes. He still resisted taking the HIV test, telling himself that if his test for other STDs came back positive, he would test for HIV. Thus when the results came back negative for syphilis and showed a good blood count and a clean urine analysis, he told himself, "all is well" (undated note; box 1, folder 8). However, as the weeks passed, Islas continued to feel uneasy, and he continued to read his body for any signs. To put his mind at ease, he decided to set up an appointment for an HIV test. He again avoided going to the Stanford University Medical Center, even though it already had a long history of blood testing for HIV (it was the first in the nation to set up blood banks in 1983). Islas set up his appointment with Dr. Babb at the Palo Alto Medical so he could keep his medical record separate from his professional life; he was afraid that if the test did not turn out favorably, Stanford University Medical Center might share his records with his department and that he would lose his job. However, when Islas finally gathered up the courage to call, the receptionist at the other end of the line told him that Dr. Babb would not be back in the office until January. Islas read Dr. Babb's absence as "a sign and felt relieved," he writes in his journal (October 13, 1987). Following this episode, Islas shared his anxieties with his therapist, Dr. Paulsen; Paulsen reassured him that his conservative sexual acts in the last seven years put him in a low-risk category; Islas records his response in his journal: "How joyful and relieved I feel. 'You can't get it that way,' he tells me and the phrase is a balm on my soul" (November 25, 1987).

But by January 1988, Islas was like a vibrating piece of glass on the verge of shattering into thousands of shards. He knew that to pacify himself, he would have to take the test, even if it meant hearing the worst; even if it meant that he would have to face his own mortality straight on; even if it meant that he would have to radically remap his sense of self and being in the world yet again, and like never before. Just before Dr. Babb was to return to the medical center in January, Islas went home to El Paso for the Christmas break to spend time with his family. Desperate to talk to a family member about his fears, he gathered the courage to talk to his father. In a journal entry dated December 23, 1987, he writes about telling his father "about my AIDS anxieties and my decision to have the antibody test." However, Islas's confession met unsympathetic ears. His father responded with cool indifference. It was the same, Islas writes, as when "I came down with polio 41 years ago. The man is impossible! How does anyone get through to someone like that?" (December 23, 1987; box 2, folder 1). When Islas returned to Palo Alto after the break, he immediately called Dr. Babb's office to set up an appointment. On January 4, 1988, Islas checked in at the front desk and waited for the on-duty nurse, Shannon Magginnis, to draw his blood for an HIV antibody test. He walked out that afternoon knowing that his blood was on its way to the testing center—knowing that he would not be able to reverse the direction of a process that would tell him with certainty the true narrative past and present of his body. A certain calm settled in as returned home from the doctor's office, writing in his journal, "I'll know in a week" (January 4, 1988).

On January 14, 1988, Dr. Babb called Islas with the test results. He had tested positive for the HIV antigens. To ensure the test's reliability, Dr. Babb recommended yet another test. Islas agreed. After another visit to the clinic for a blood draw, Dr. Babb sent Islas's blood for more testing. A week later, Islas received a print-out from Virunostics Clinical Laboratories in San Francisco: the box marked "positive" was checked. Islas's fear was confirmed (box 1, folder 8). "The horrors begin," he writes in his journal on January 14, 1988 (box 2, folder 1). No matter what psychological preparation Islas had made for this news, the reality overpowered him: he was HIV-positive. His body was being colonized by an invisible presence that would lead to a defenseless immune system and death. Now he could imagine—and almost feel—the virus working under the cover of his skin, disarming his fighter cells from being able to fend off foreign invaders. Suddenly, the world was turned upside down. Islas could no longer trust his body.

Everything seemed to stop. Whether he had a year or five years to live, his life appeared to shrink, he describes, "to the end of a telescope—the small end" (January 15, 1988; box 2, folder 1); it was no longer the expansive space he imagined it to be, the space that would allow him to fulfill his dreams. After Dr. Babb prescribed medication to clear Islas's nasal passages, he writes in his journal, "Symbolically, I see this as the beginning and weep and weep with Ken and Nora" (February 8, 1988). Islas's body and its different textures no longer indicated to him either the absence or the presence of disease but registered instead the rate at which he saw himself moving closer to death: "I am noticing mole-like, dark spots in places that make me wonder. Have they been there before and I just didn't notice? They fill me with fear and dread" (April 6, 1988).

Islas blamed himself for contracting HIV, but he also felt angry about the double-standard that excoriated homosexual promiscuity while winking at heterosexual promiscuity. In one of his lectures at Stanford during this period, he criticized Hemingway's straight characters because they have, he writes, "sex without paying for it" and are never considered a "contamination" (Hemingway lecture; box 23, folder 12). He struggled not to internalize the heterosexist view, to see himself as a "diseased" gay Chicano, forced to inhabit both sites of visibility and sites of invisibility in a society that feared death by the "wrong" means. Yet, he could not help slipping into moments when he would reread his earlier sexual adventures not as acts of gay emancipation, but as sinful and criminal behavior that deserved punishment. He experienced bouts of paralysis, often feeling that he could not move his "legs and lips as if underwater" (January 27, 1988; box 2, folder 1). He also began to disassociate self from body: "I am not my body. I am not my consciousness, I am not my feelings and ideas" (March 18, 1988).

Islas came to understand time differently. No longer able to take time for granted, he became determined to do everything he could to stretch it out as much as possible. To expand time—and relieve social anxiety and his feeling of being sexually crippled—Islas turned more forcefully to his writing. He attacked *Migrant Souls*—the sequel to *The Rain God*—at a frenzied pace. As with his earlier physical challenges, first with polio and later with colitis, he used his writing to externalize and thereby control his psychic pain. After several months of writing with furious speed, he realized that he could not keep his thoughts of his "diseased" body at bay. He writes in his journal, for example, "Morning demons are back. . . . I am also afraid that my books will not see the light of day before I have to focus on my body" (October 24, 1988; box 2, folder 1). Islas finished *Migrant Souls* less because of his editor's attentive prodding and more because writing the book worked well as a strategy to transform into art—that is, to externalize—the suffering and pain that would otherwise have devastated him.

Islas also turned to books—especially autobiographies and spiritual meditations. He read, for example, the autobiography of the early twentieth-century French activist/philosopher/spiritualist Simone Weil, who had been similarly plagued with a lifetime of health problems. Weil's *Attente de dieu* (1950) offered Islas some respite from the feelings of guilt that plagued him, a context for his suffering: "Am I to be a saint after all? I see myself as the 'bad' thief. He suffered, too" (journal, April 26, 1988; box 2, folder 1). He also read gay Jungian psychologist John Fortunato's *Embracing the Exile* (1982), which helped him to reformulate his Catholic conceptual framework so that he could embrace his identity as a gay Chicano. And Islas found solace in friend, colleague, and writer Nancy Packer's *In My Father's House* (1988)—an autobiographical account of surviving childhood sexual abuse. These were just a few of the many books Islas read to explore his own life story in a more universal light and to help himself achieve greater enlightenment on what he considered the last leg of his journey.

Family also became a source of support. He felt most comfortable revealing his status to his brother Mario (who was at this time out as a gay priest), "asking/praying to have the terror removed [and asking to] have *my spirit* healed" (journal, January 18, 1988; box 2, folder 1). Islas knew that he would need the support of the rest of his family, so during a trip to El Paso in March 1988, he told them the news through what he described as "the filter of mortality" (journal, March 19, 1988; box 2, folder 1). They readily accepted him with love and affection.

Whenever Islas felt well enough, he would try to maintain a "regular" life. He continued to keep a regular writing and teaching schedule as well as grading and commenting on honors theses and dissertations. He even managed to fit in a weeklong trip to Paris. His bouts of good health, however, were becoming shorter and shorter. By the summer of 1989, Islas's life had become, as he had feared before his diagnosis, more and more focused on the illness, an ordeal centered on taking large quantities of AZT, scheduling in Alpha Interferon, and monitoring white blood counts. He no longer marked as exceptions those moments when he was sick; the exception was now the rare moment when he was feeling well. After recovering from pneumonia in the summer of 1990, he writes in his journal, "I am gradually coming back to life. What a summer siege! Hope I am spared that in future. But there is no future, is there, for any of us? Only today. And today is good" (August 30, 1990; box 53, folder 5).

He was very ill when he returned to Palo Alto after a Christmas visit to El Paso in 1990. On February 15, 1991, he died in his bedroom, finally crossing the threshold of death that had haunted his life from early childhood. His ashes were scattered in the Pacific and in the El Paso desert to honor his deep sense of the cyclical nature of life and death. Islas's lifelong struggle with a sense of being physically and socially mis-embodied had come to an end.

FIVE Being Chicano

Islas's identity was very much informed by his cultural and racial sense of being Mexican and American. He was born to second-generation Catholic Mexican Americans and raised within the cultural and socioeconomic U.S./Mexico borderlands. He grew up where Mexican and Anglo bodies rubbed up against one another, where tacos and hamburgers appeared at the same dinner table, and where Spanish and English commingled; and Islas had a deep sense of himself as Mexican and American. Though he was phenotypically light enough to "pass" as Anglo, his family's strong cultural heritage, their own spectrum of different Mexican phenotypes, and his inhabiting of a Mexican/Anglo border space firmly anchored in him a fluid yet definite sense of self as Mexican American—and as "Chicano" from the late 1960s onward. Indeed, his layered sense of being Mexican American (and later "Chicano") informed the way he inhabited, complicated, and transformed—and in turn was inhabited, complicated, and transformed by—a variety of culturally, racially, and historically circumscribed spaces. As Islas once lectured to a group of undergraduates, he, like many of them, was a racialized being firmly anchored in "history—both political and literary as well as personal" (Mark Twain lecture; box 25, folder 20). As noted in chapter 1, Islas's sense of Mexicanness was strongly influenced by his paternal grandmother, Crecenciana, who instilled in him a pride in his "Spanish" heritage that he would recognize as myth only much later in life: his light skin, his *puro* Spanish, his flawless English. Islas would explore this paradigm of internalized racism in his writing; and in his sensitivity to the problem of internalized racism, he was ahead of his time. He had to negotiate a path in a complex social world, first in El Paso, as a light-skinned Mexican American, and then in Palo Alto, as a Chicano. In this negotiation, we hear the more public voice of Islas, first as a boy living in the U.S./Mexican borderlands, and later as Chicano scholar, professor, and mentor. His contributions are all the more remarkable in view of the inner doubts he wrestled with.

OUT OF THE BARRIO

Islas spent his early childhood at the margin of the southside Mexican section of El Paso known as El Segundo Barrio. His family had lived in this part of town since his grandparents migrated to the United States in the late 1910s; it was a stone's throw from the border to the south and a safe distance from the city's central business district, with its banks and boutiques that served the wealthier Anglos who lived in the northern outskirts. Islas's family lived just on the other side of the tracks from El Segundo Barrio. His neighborhood was not quite Mexican town and not quite the Anglo district; it was a place where Mexican Americans, African Americans, and some older Anglos lived. Most struggled to survive by working in the Anglo-owned steel, rail, coal, and cement industries. As a young boy, Islas would hear as much Spanish as English on the streets; he would see walking in the streets both "Mexicans and blacks," he tells his students in a lecture on minority voices in American literature (Chicano literature lecture; box 32, folder 15). For the most part, as a young boy Islas never had to venture far from what was called "little Mexico"— that part of town ignored by the city's Anglo elite. Little Mexico was a womb space where children like Islas were looked after by the tight-knit, extended family community. Little Mexico would become visible to the Anglos only when contractors needed workers or when the city's police force would invade the neighborhood to contain the city's "criminal" element, especially pachucos and zoot-suiters. Mexican Americans like Islas's uncle Enrique called himself a pachuco and a zoot-suiter, proudly displaying his difference from a U.S. mainstream and his parents' Mexican heritage by walking the streets with a bold swagger and wearing baggy "drapes" (pants) and wide-shouldered jackets. The bodies, culture, and language that flowed through the streets instilled in Islas a deep affiliation with Mexico culturally and racially.

For young Islas, the borders between the barrio and surrounding neighborhoods were somewhat porous. Islas and his family could buy groceries and clothes in the *barrio*-run *tiendas* and get haircuts at the Mexican-run barbershop; but they could also venture into the central business district, as Islas often did with his grandmother Crecenciana or his mother. They saw the "We Don't Serve Mexicans" signs in the shop windows, but with their fair skin and good English, they passed through doors that otherwise might have remained closed to them.

Strong family support for Islas's bicultural education would also open doors for him. His grandmother Crecenciana taught him to speak, read, and write English at an early age. His parents insisted that he attend an English-speaking elementary school, but they encouraged him to read and write in Spanish at home. This rich educational experience not only opened doors for Islas as a young boy, but also provided the path for his journey into a complex, multicultural sense of self. At a young age, he could read Spanish or English books at the library. At elementary school, where he was known as "Art," his fluency in Spanish and English meant that he did not have to endure the linguistic ostracism suffered by classmates who did not speak English. His experiences of the different worlds of El Paso multiplied—the library, his English-only school, visits to down-

town, life in and around the barrio—and his world expanded, along with
his sense of inhabiting a culturally layered, urban borderland. At home he
would hear stories in Spanish and English, while at the library he would
read books that were authored by European and Anglo American writers
and populated with characters who, though white, did not distance him
from his own experience as a nonwhite subject. As his imagination ex-
panded around these multiply layered cultural storyscapes, he experi-
enced and witnessed El Paso not as an apartheid border city, but as a
world that offered the possibility of a new imaginative blend of Mexican
and American. Later, as an adult writing his book *La Mollie and the King of
Tears,* he invented just such a character, Louie Mendoza, who sees the
world through a hybridizing lens. Louie, for example, reads Hamlet as a
Chicano bad-boy; *Hamlet,* Louie says, is "Shakespeare's version of *High
Noon* with a big swordout instead of a shootout at the end" (box 8, folder
1). Islas's bilingual education and multicultural imagination opened his
eyes to a world of possibility, giving him the passport he needed to travel
back and forth between El Paso's Anglo and Mexican worlds. As a young
boy in the 1940s, he saw but did not see the "We Don't Serve Mexicans"
signs in the shop windows, the drinking fountain signs, the signs pro-
hibiting Mexican Americans from swimming in the public swimming
pool except on "Mexican day"—the day before it was cleaned.

The racial climate in El Paso had improved somewhat by the early
1950s, when Islas was a teenager. With Mexican Americans becoming a
demographic majority (and many, like Islas's family, entering the middle
class), organizations like LULAC put pressure on public policy makers to
desegregate schools and implement bilingual education programs. Shop
and restaurant window signs prohibiting Mexicans and African Ameri-
cans from entering began to disappear; there were no longer separate
drinking fountains for Anglos and Others; there was more interracial
mingling on the sidewalks.

At El Paso High, with its increasingly diverse student body, Islas's
well-practiced ability to move between cultural and linguistic communi-
ties paid off. Because of his fluency in English and light skin, he could
enter at will the Anglo clique; and because of his fluency in Spanish and
the hybrid Spanish/English slang, *caló* (spoken by his father at home), he

was accepted into the Mexican American collective. His accentless fluency in the Anglo and Mexican American languages and cultures granted him equal access to these social spaces as well as those tangentially connected: the minor but very actively present Jewish and Syrian student collectives. As his popularity across groups proved, Islas's bicultural/bilingual upbringing allowed him to step into the limelight of a multicultural wave that was beginning to sweep across the high school and El Paso generally. At one point, Islas and his Jewish and Syrian peers organized an extracurricular group that promoted multicultural awareness and recognized the cultural interests and educational needs of the Mexican Americans, Jews, and Syrians at the high school. Islas playfully recalls this period, writing how "some of us formed a group called the 'kosher Catholics' in which out of respect for each other's beliefs, we ate neither ham sandwiches nor meat on Fridays" (California State Teachers of English lecture; box 29, folder 3). The organization was not formally recognized by the high school, but Islas and his polyglot colleagues met regularly to discuss ways to expand interracial and intercultural awareness and promote cross-racial bridges of solidarity and empowerment.

As Islas was enjoying social and academic success at school, his family's fortunes were improving, too. His parents' frugal manner of living combined with increases in salaries meant that they could afford to move from Almagordo Street to a "better" part of town. So when Islas returned home from high school at the end of the day, instead heading toward the southern part of the city, he made his way to the northerly outskirts of El Paso, to a suburban-style home surrounded by middle-class Anglo and Jewish families. The combined salaries of his mother, who continued to work as a secretary for a local cement factory, and his father, who worked as policeman, meant that Islas could enjoy the comforts of a middle-class life, including more space for his much-needed moments of privacy. Of course, the family's socioeconomic rise did not mean that El Paso had suddenly become a race-friendly city. Arturo Islas Sr. finally made the rank of inspector, but only after over thirty-five years on the force, hitting many a glass ceiling. Of course, it did not help that, as Earl Shorris recollects of Arturo Islas Sr., he lacked a certain finesse "in dealing with superiors in his own department: When he felt he was ill-treated in some way . . . , he did not hesitate to advise the person who has wronged him to 'kiss the Mexican side of my ass,' even if that person was the chief of police" (1992, 100). Though Islas's parents still had to contend with racism in El Paso, as Islas told a group of undergraduates at Stanford during a lecture in 1971, "the sense that they were better off than their parents made my parents able to ignore the political and social injustices they suffered. After all, they could reason, 'we're better off' (meaning economically) than our parents, and our children will be better off than we. For them, the American dream in its economic sense was working" (Minority voices in American literature lecture; box 32, folder 15). The family's upward mobility opened up the possibility for Islas and his younger brothers to live in and move between the different social and racial spaces that made up El Paso, and later, between similar spaces at college in California (Arturo and Louie) and seminary in Kansas (Mario).

Bilingualism was key to the Islas family's success. One of Jovita's most important roles as a secretary at the cement factory was to be a liaison between the Spanish-speaking workers and the Anglo bosses. Arturo Sr. used his bilingual skill to mediate between the largely Anglo police department and the Spanish-speaking community. For the Islas family, as well as other (especially bilingual) Mexican Americans, the 1950s was a period of socioeconomic empowerment. The young Islas was a beneficiary of this opening of social and economic opportunities, and he experienced El Paso as a nurturing environment. Later, he would become more aware of his privilege—and aware that his family's upward mobility entailed some cost, both to themselves and to those Mexican Americans who were left behind in the struggle to realize the American dream. In a lecture at Stanford, Islas later recalled that his family's upward mobility led to a "regular neglect of their sorrier kin, disregard of elders, and scorn for race and creed in public and private, as well as in Cesar Salad and roast beef instead of *pozole* and *gorditas*" (Nabokov's *Lolita* lecture; box 25, folder 9).

A CHICANO IN THE IVORY TOWER

When Islas entered Stanford as a freshman in the fall of 1956, race relations and politics in the United States were changing—for better and for worse.

Many working-class and middle-class Mexican Americans had begun to galvanize around issues of desegregation and bilingual education, but their efforts were met with strong Anglo resistance. And, at the level of national policy making, the government sustained laws that treated Americans of Mexican descent as raw labor with no civil rights. Islas looked back on this period with mixed feelings, remembering the anger and frustration his family felt when, for example, Eisenhower's administration resumed "operation wetback," which deported any Spanish-surnamed person who could not immediately prove U.S. citizenship. The Mexican American demand for basic civil liberties—equal access to education, the right to organize, and fair political representation—was becoming more visible as a politicized collective, but local and national administrations continued to block any large political advances.

Ironically, it was within the walls of Stanford's ivory tower, void of racial diversity or sense of community, that Islas experienced the freedom to choose how to define his role in a racially conflicted United States. Islas was one of a few racial minorities admitted to Stanford in 1956; long before Affirmative Action (admission "quotas" had only just begun to include Jews and women), he beat the odds and was the first Mexican American admitted as an undergraduate. Winning an Alfred P. Sloan scholarship based on high school achievement, Islas left the desert and his Mexican American environs behind and entered Stanford's well-manicured, lushly green, palm-tree-filled campus, with its majority WASP student body. At the time, Islas was one of two "minority" students—the other was an African American woman—in an entering class of one thousand. He recalls how he was "scared and lonely and totally bewildered and overwhelmed by this strange, cold (anything not like the desert where I grew up seemed cold to me) place" (Casa Zapata lecture; box 29, folder 24). Stanford proved to be "cold" in more ways than one. Islas immediately felt, he later recollects, "estranged and bewildered by the Stanford way of life," which was given shape by a mass of white, upper-middle-class students (Casa Zapata lecture). When Islas identified himself as "Mexican American," students assumed, since the Latinos at Stanford were wealthy exchange students, that he was a son of a diplomat from somewhere in Latin America. He felt alienated and out of place.

Yet it was within the "cold," alienating Stanford campus that Islas began to become more conscious of his racial identity. As he progressed through college, he maintained his strong identification as a Mexican American from the Southwest, and he was encouraged by what seemed to be great tectonic shifts in the campus's racial demographic. Though Islas did not belong to a fraternity, in the spring of 1957 he supported the fraternity association's passing of a resolution to oppose racial and religious discrimination. (One such fraternity had its charter rescinded after pledging four Jewish men in 1961.) And, he began to discover some literature that spoke to his own experience, such as the 1959 publication of José Antonio Villarreal's autobiography, *Pocho*. During Islas's final year as an undergraduate, he began to take notice, too, of the political changes and organizations in California and the Southwest generally. Though he was never the type to march in the streets (partly due to his limp), he took note of and supported Mexican American organizations that sought more equitable political representation and civil rights. For example, he followed closely and supported MAPA (Mexican American Political Association). And, in 1960, when he entered Stanford's English PhD program, he actively supported and voted for John F. Kennedy Jr., who was strongly supported by Mexican Americans.

Islas's early years as a graduate student were filled with political and social tremors that would later become the explosive countercultural movements and civil rights activism of the late 1960s. In his third year as a PhD student, he signed petitions and helped organize student protests against U.S. policy toward Cuba in 1963. In 1964, he actively supported student demands that the administration appoint a faculty administration committee on educational opportunities for disadvantaged minorities to recruit and retain Mexican American, African American, and other minority students. In the spring of 1964, he gathered along with hundreds of other Stanford students to hear the inspiring words of Martin Luther King on civil rights. He also participated in the Vietnam protests on campus and the forming of the campus organization Stanford Sexual Rights Forum to raise awareness of gay/lesbian and bisexual students. Islas's political and racial awareness was deepened, too, by the discovery of writers John Rechy and James Baldwin. Islas was struck by John

Rechy's chronicling of a queer Mexican-Scottish American character from El Paso in his best-selling *City of Night*, and he became an avid reader of all of James Baldwin's novels and journalistic essays.

By the end of the 1967 school year, though, Islas was disenchanted with academics, describing Stanford as a "creature of vested interests and dead tradition [filled with] automatism, snobbery, and prejudice, and so little pertinence to the real needs of men" (American lives lecture; box 27, folder 3). Islas did not drop out, like many of his Anglo cohorts, to participate in the hippie resistance to the capitalist work ethic and the institutional control of mind/body, but rather to be able to find a job that would actively engage with "the real needs of men." Among the various jobs he held during this period, he worked at the Menlo Park V.A. hospital as a speech therapist for African American, Anglo, and Mexican American veterans; later he supported the student and worker protests in Prague over the Soviet Union's invasion of Czechoslovakia in 1968, and also the student protests in Mexico City (what became known as the "Tlatelolco Massacre") just before the Olympic Games in October of that year. He was drawn to the activism that was spreading across campuses, the nation, and the world: the walkouts in east Los Angeles that resulted in police brutality against Mexican Americans, the Kent State protests against the Nixon administration's invasion of Cambodia, and the Chicano labor protests in the central valley. (Islas remained an active supporter of the United Farm Workers throughout his life.)

After living and working for a year and a half away from Stanford, Islas felt that he should return to finish his dissertation, envisioning a career in teaching. He would help the "real needs of men" by becoming a teacher. As a strongly self-identified Chicano, he would mentor Chicano/a students and revise the curriculum to showcase Mexican American contributions to the humanities. He knew that he could fight a more lasting battle as teacher and writer with the goal of carving paths for future generations of Chicanos/as in higher education.[1] With encouragement from Ian Watt, Islas returned to Stanford in January 1969.

CHICANO INVASION

By the time Islas returned to campus, the university had changed visibly. The administration's policy to grant African Americans and Chicanos priority in obtaining financial aid increased the numbers of students of color: over fifty Chicanos/as and over seventy African Americans (compared with the three admitted, for example, when Islas began his PhD in 1960) were now matriculated. And in the fall of 1969, an African and Afro-American studies major was established with fifteen faculty affiliates and thirteen sophomores and juniors (eight black, five white) signed on as majors. The curriculum now included ethnic writers as required reading for freshmen—Claude Brown's *Manchild in the Promised Land*, Eldridge Cleaver's *Soul on Ice*, and the *Autobiography of Malcolm X*.

Islas was pleased with the reforms, but knew more could be done—especially in the area of making visible and institutionalizing the field of Chicano literary studies. African American writers had made it onto syllabi lists (albeit minimally), but Islas noticed the marked absence of Chicano voices. Heartened when neighboring University of California-Berkeley published the first Chicano literary journal, *El Grito*, Islas was inspired to launch a similar one.[2] However, to be in a position to start literary journals and mentor the fresh Chicano/a arrivals, he knew that he would have to finish writing his dissertation. This was slowed down by his ill health, but he managed to finish in 1971.

As Islas finished his dissertation, a space opened up in the English department—that place Islas dreamed of working to wage his cultural battles. Hired as an assistant professor in 1971, Islas chose to teach as his first freshman English seminar a course on Chicano literature. The class filled fast, with over twenty Chicanos/as in attendance. Students were required to write and then critically analyze their own creative writing, and Islas encouraged them to speak from their own experience as Chicanos/as. This was one of many small steps Islas made to help Stanford to, he writes, "recognize the existence of Mexican people in this country [and acknowledge positively] the differences in cultures between North American and Mexican American" (Los Angeles alumni lecture, box 29, folder 24). Of course, while some professors and administrators supported the effort to put African Americans and Chicanos on the cultural map, many at Stanford did not approve. Islas learned quickly that he would have to use the master's tools to rebuild—gradually—the master's house. He knew that to make visible traditionally marginal and/or invisible knowledge systems, he would have to learn strategies for subtly bending the curriculum around and through a corpus of Chicano texts. The goal, he declares, was to enable "another different and worthy imagination to express itself as itself" (Los Angeles alumni lecture). He knew that he would have to perform acrobatic feats; he would simultaneously teach Western and non-Western "views of humanity together and retain what is valuable in both" to rebuild the master's house (Los Angeles alumni lecture).

He also knew that he could not achieve this without knowing how to play the administration, learning to ingratiate himself with the "significant players on the administration, like the president" to make deft, behind-the-scenes maneuvers that would alter the curriculum and push the administration to hire more faculty of color (interview with Cecilia Burciaga). Several weeks after Islas went to then-president Richard W. Lyman to convince him of the university's lack of faculty diversity, Lyman responded to Islas in a letter, "As we are both too painfully aware, the necessary changes for our minority community are not going to be apparent overnight" (box 30, folder 15). Islas knew that to change the curriculum and also change administrative procedure for recruitment, he would need the strength of large numbers. Eventually, Islas did see several new hires that would build up the base of support necessary for curriculum reform. By 1972, eight Chicano faculty (no women) and eleven staff members (three women) had joined Stanford—double the number from 1971. Later in the decade Islas and other newly recruited Chicano faculty such as Renato Rosaldo, Jerry Porras, and Jim Leckie successfully pushed the administration to create an "assistant to the president for Chicano affairs" position, which was filled by Cecilia Burciaga, who fought long and hard to make Chicano/a issues visible on campus. With a representative in the administration, the voices of Chicano students and faculty would finally be heard.

As an assistant professor without tenure, Islas was careful to make changes that would ultimately garner support from the department and administration. His pedagogy, scholarship, and creative writing eventually won him tenure in March 1976, thus securing his livelihood and his place within the university. As a tenured professor, he could critique university policies more openly, without fear of dismissal. In a 1979 presentation to the Stanford administration, Islas and his fellow Chicano faculty members asserted that Chicanos/as "would be the majority group in the state of California by the end of the century" (box 30, folder 15). In the same presentation, they demanded that the university formally institute "an academically coherent, research-oriented program in Chicano, Mexican-American or Mexican studies." In response to social, racial, and economic changes nationwide, they demanded that the university acknowledge "the ethnic group that will in the next decade become the largest minority contingent in the nation." Stanford could hardly ignore the facts, and the administration funded the Center for Chicano Studies—a Chicano/a think tank that would become one of the principal centers for Chicano research in the nation.

As a Chicano professor at Stanford in the 1970s, Islas witnessed the push-and-pull tug between leftist activism and right-wing conservatism. The administration, which had traditionally bowed to the wishes of an elite white trustee board, did begin to take notice of Islas's and others' efforts to establish affirmative action recruitment and retention policies. The voices asking for reform could not be ignored. Television coverage of campus activism cast the administration in an unfavorable light, often showing club-wielding police battalions armed with tear gas to disband student protests. So when Richard W. Lyman took over as president from Kenneth S. Pitzer in the fall of 1970, Stanford knew it needed to handle its political image with care and dexterity. So, though President Lyman identified Islas and his small cohort of Chicanos as performing, in Islas's words, a "guerrilla theater of war" that made the university unsafe for "learning and debate" (Dinkelspiel Award lecture; box 30, folder 16), the university heard and at least partially met many of their demands. The Stanford administration feared being labeled as reactionary and unable to move with the changing social and political tides of the nation. As a result, Lyman's decade-long administration did implement some of the pro-minority faculty and student demands.

As mentioned earlier, Islas did not position himself at the front lines of the "guerrilla theatre of war"; rather, he sought to gain the ear of those with power, like Lyman and others high up in the administration. With a few strategically placed faculty like Islas, who represented the front-line activist students and faculty, much was changed. The use of the Indian "Prince Lightfoot" as the university's mascot was banned in 1972; moreover, the number of American Indians had increased to fifty-seven undergraduate and twenty-two graduate students by 1973; and financial support was provided for retention activities. And, while it took most of the 1970s for Islas and other faculty and staff to force the administration to drop its admission procedure requiring applicants to send photographs along with their application, this was finally done at the end of the decade. Though the administration was reluctant to agree, Islas and others argued that this procedure had long been used to ensure unofficially the continued legacy of a "healthy" looking—Anglo—student body.

Islas felt immersed in a similar tug-of-war between the push for increased social, cultural, and racial awareness and the pull toward a conservative, rightist agenda nationally. While there was much to celebrate in terms of Chicanos/as finally being recognized as a significant presence and producer of culture in the United States, Islas noticed much continued hostility toward brown people. He was especially attuned to the way in which the media sensationally misrepresented the Mexicano/Chicano. An avid reader of the *New York Review of Books*, Islas was shocked when he read an article by John Womack Jr. titled "Who Are the Chicanos?" (August 31, 1972), a diatribe against Chicano activists such as César Chávez. Womack, who had published a highly acclaimed and widely sold biography of the Mexican revolutionary hero Emiliano Zapata, scorned the effort of Chicanos who sought to make visible their cultural presence and their labor in building the nation. Womack identified Chicano activists as a "hustling and strapped" group of people who feel that "their kind has suffered more than any other kind of people in America [and] that only prejudice keeps them from getting more out of the country" (box 33, folder 5). Islas identified with those that Womack labeled as "amateur chiefs," whose political rhetoric, Womack wrote, would never succeed in attaining "their quota of revenge and power in America" (box 33, folder 5).

So, while Islas witnessed certain progress in racial awareness, he faced daily reminders of the racist psychology of the nation at large. He noted the way the *San Francisco Chronicle* pathologized Mexicans, clipping an article published on May 3, 1974, that read: "The tens of thousands of Mexicans who *sneak* into the United States each month can dodge the immigration patrols. But they are often trapped by a common problem: *illness*" (box 33, folder 5; emphasis his). Islas was struck by the reporter's use of hyperbole to describe how the Mexican invasion threatened to "spread contagious diseases through the rest of the population" and the writer's final recommendation to report anyone suspected of being illegal "or face felony charges with a possible $2000 fine and five-year prison sentence." At times, Islas could not help but feel that his struggle to guarantee equal rights for all Chicanos, African Americans, American Indians, and Asian Americans was futile in a xenophobic nation whose mainstream felt threatened by the racial Other.

In a department that considered Hemingway and Fitzgerald marginal figures within an English undergraduate curriculum of study, Islas bent curricular expectations and began to teach the first Chicano/a literature courses at Stanford. His charismatic presence and skill as a teacher helped put multiethnic literature on the curricular map at Stanford. In 1976, he was given the prestigious Lloyd Dinkelspiel Award for his "sage counsel and warm-hearted leadership" within the Chicano community at Stanford (box 30, folder 16). By the end of the 1970s, "in a spirit of educating the imagination," Islas had popularized Chicano/a literature classes and had demonstrated that ethnic and Chicano/a cultural contributions "can be ignored no longer by the United States" (Casa Zapata lecture). Islas was instrumental in the transformation of an otherwise all-white, Euro-American literary curriculum, and he inspired others to teach courses that included a wide range of voices: African American, Asian American, American Indian, and Chicano/a. Moving into the 1980s and the decade of the culture wars on university campuses nationwide, Stanford's curriculum committee began to look to Islas and other faculty of color to overhaul core courses like Western Civilization, which was required of all freshmen. Such a course, as Islas remarks during an interview, "provided a view of Western civilization and the humanities in the minds of our undergraduate students that totally excluded the history and imagination of entire races of people who existed in this hemisphere before they were 'discovered' by some of those very figures in Western civilization we were taught to study and admire" (José Antonio Burciaga interview, November 28, 1990).

THE CULTURE WARS

As Islas moved into the new decade, the university was being forced to radically alter its racial makeup and curriculum. Several months after President Lyman resigned, in January 1980, Islas found himself having to learn how to gain the ear of the newly appointed president, Don Kennedy. As it turned out, Kennedy was attentive to proactive curricular and admission demands. As then-president for Chicano Affairs Cecilia Burciaga recalls, "It was a wonderful time, the golden age for minorities" (interview with Cecilia Burciaga). More wide-reaching affirmative action policies of recruitment and retention were instituted, more ethnicity-based residential houses appeared on campus to accommodate the growing number of minority students, and a Euro-American curriculum was overhauled. Islas zealously applauded these advances, which contributed "to the education of all our undergraduates" (Burciaga interview). The steady in-flow of increasing numbers of Chicanos, African Americans, Asians, and women on campus made Islas hopeful that "minorities" as token racial representatives at Stanford would soon be a fact of the past.

While Kennedy's administration admitted more minority students than prior administrations, Islas was fearful that it would not follow through with building an infrastructure to sustain these students and foster an enduring multicultural/multiethnic legacy. That the administration did not open up the necessary tenure-track professor lines to answer this need meant that the few like Islas were forced to carry heavy teaching and mentoring workloads. Islas saw it as the university's way to appease the demands of affirmative action while setting it up to fail. As the 1980s progressed, Islas saw his fellow faculty of color experience deep exhaustion from work overloads. He also saw increasing flare-ups of reactionary sentiment on campus toward minority issues. Anglo students who had in the past kept quiet about racial issues were screaming reverse-prejudice and complaining loudly about the injustices of affirmative action and feelings of exclusion from ethnic organizations. The ethnicity-based houses that Islas had helped institutionalize, like Casa Zapata, were suddenly under attack. After Islas expressed his upset over the possible removal of some of these houses, then-president Don Kennedy responded in a letter to Islas how some houses would be disbanded because, he writes, "our system is saturated with themes" (March 18, 1981; box 2, folder 1). In an interview with José Antonio Burciaga, Islas speaks of this reaction to the houses as reflective of an everyday America where the population at large do not want to be reminded that they have, he says, "annihilated people and/or stolen their lands" (November 28, 1990).

As the decade unfolded, Islas watched as faculty, students, and administration at Stanford became polarized between a political left and right. The two sides entered a battle that eventually placed Stanford at the epicenter of what became known nationally as the "great books debate" or "the culture wars." Reactionaries galvanized around the idea that Western culture was crumbling at the hands of liberal intellectuals like Islas—throwbacks, in their mind, from a 1960s civil rights sensibility. An increasingly bold and vocal conservative right considered multiculturalism the ultimate threat to a Western tradition whose canonical great white authors established the standards of "objectivity" and "truth." For such detractors, multiculturalism spelled cultural relativism to an anarchic degree.

In the centrifuge that would spin Toni Morrison and Ernesto Galarza to one side and Plato and Aristotle to the other, Islas's attempt to complicate the Chicano/a cultural terrain was perceived as one such direct threat to Western culture and civilization. By 1986, Islas found himself at the center of what was becoming a vast ideological dispute that was spreading across the nation. In 1987, the Reverend Jesse Jackson and his rainbow coalition arrived on the Stanford campus to promote affirmative action and to reform curricular needs: "Hey, hey, ho, ho! Western Culture's gotta go!" they chanted. A year later, William Bennett visited the campus, countering Jackson by proclaiming the need to study the "great books" and likening affirmative action to a "malignant mutation." During this period, E. D. Hirsch came out of his conservative hibernation with the publication of *Cultural Literacy*, which further pathologized the liberal left's project to diversify the curriculum as a disease that, if left to follow its own course, would infect and destroy Western culture entirely. And, *Closing of the American Mind* made professor Alan Bloom an overnight best-seller and celebrity among those on the right.

In the late-1980s conservative milieu, Islas was targeted as one of many liberals responsible for the moral, intellectual, and social decay of civilization. Of course, Islas had known of the presence of the Blooms and Bennetts for a long time. Such figures existed even among the ethnically marginalized. When Richard Rodriguez published *Hunger of Memory* in 1982, Islas was quick to comment that "the greatest irony about this book is that it will be read not so much by the *gringos* whose society *Richheard* wants so desperately to be admitted to but rather by those very beneficiaries of affirmative action and bilingual programs who are now beginning to populate universities in increasing numbers" (book review; box 31, folder 2). Islas was similarly taken aback when the African American Stanford research fellow Thomas Sowell published *The Economics and Politics of Race,* in which he argues that affirmative action hurts minority students. As voices from the racial margins who had become darlings of the right, Rodriguez and Sowell were particularly damaging to Islas's progressive multiculturalist agenda. They had become the visible authorities on what was wrong—not what was right—about affirmative action and bilingual education practices in the United States.

Islas had grown used to encountering a mainstream that maintained a love/hate attitude toward Chicanos/as. On the one hand, the 1980s marked a renaissance in Chicano/Latino culture: Edward James Olmos appeared in *Miami Vice, Stand and Deliver*; Luis Valdez's film *La Bamba* grossed a record $53 million; and Los Lobos, Lisa Lisa, and Miami Sound

Machine made it into the top ten on the music charts. And of Latino authors, Islas wrote how the northeast was beginning to discuss them "with respect and admiration in the periodicals that are considered worthy and widely distributed. We see the names of these writers alongside the names of the writers, young and old, who are revered in North America" (Latin American writers' conference lecture; box 29, folder 9). On the other hand, negative images of brown people were common in the media, and a "model minority" like Richard Rodriguez was acclaimed, Islas laments, for writing "an autobiography in which he excoriates any academic who favors affirmative action and bilingual education programs, even though he himself reaped the benefits of such programs in his own education" (Latin American writers' conference lecture). Islas regarded the 1980s as a tragic moment that marked "a crisis in the representation of people from my background within the literary community of the nation" (Latin American writers' conference lecture).

For Islas, all the eighties hype around Latino culture spicing up the American mainstream was a smoke screen hiding the everyday racism that continued to disenfranchise and exploit brown bodies:

> The country at large continues to see us with disdain or, as most often happens, to ignore us altogether. When they look at the goings-on South of the Border, the focus is on drugs and debts (with little or no nodding toward our part in the creation of such monstrosities) and the need to reinforce our side of the Border so as to keep the dreaded "aliens" out. Except of course, when we need them to harvest the food we eat, take care of our children, clean our houses and offices and do all those jobs considered too menial and unimportant in the modern world. And that's how we exist in the imagination of this country and the very real forces that decide what this country needs: as gardeners, maids, gang members, migrant works, drug-addicted high school dropouts, resident or illegal "aliens." (Latin American writers' conference lecture)

Islas was critical of a United States that both exploited brown bodies as laboring parts and likened those bodies to a disease that threatened to contaminate the mainstream. He reflected on the grand irony of the right's argument for reason and objectivity in the culture wars. In his view, the conservative mind-set was one in which "truth seems to have no place or importance." The eighties generally, he concludes, "is a great time for the liars, the frivolous, the greedy" (Latin American writers' conference lecture). Finally, at the close of the 1980s Islas heard a speech by S. I. Hayakawa—whose book *Language, Thought, Action* had provided Islas with a model for civil rights activism in the 1960s—in which Hayakawa, a new convert to right-wing conservatism, spoke out against immigration, especially that of Mexicans. The speech presented a "damning view of the illegal aliens from Mexico," reflecting the seemingly hopeless struggle for racial equality in the United States (Latin American writers' conference lecture).

In spite of his depressed spirits—at this point, exacerbated by his struggle with various HIV-related illnesses—Islas continued to nurture scholars that he knew would honor his legacy. He helped shape undergraduate theses that linked Chicano/a and Anglo American literature, as with Margo Ponce's thesis on the poet Lorna Dee Cervantes (box 46, folder 14). He oversaw work by upcoming Chicana PhD scholars like Febe Portillo and Bernice Zamora ("Mythopoetics of Chicano Poetry: An Introduction to Chicano Archetypes") and helped shape Gloria Velásquez-Treviño's "Cultural Ambivalence in Early Chicana Narrative." He guided Chicano poets such as Ben Sáenz and Francisco X. Alarcón. He broadened Chicano/a scholarship to include North and South American literature, which fed into José David Saldívar's visionary *Dialectics of Our Americas.* He also guided other young Chicano scholars, like Rafael Pérez-Torres, who have since emerged as leaders in the field of Chicano/a literary scholarship.

RE-ARCHITEXTURING THE MASTER'S HOUSE

Islas knew that he would never effect change if he tried to bully those in power at Stanford. From his early days as an assistant professor right up through the 1980s culture wars, he was very careful and strategic about how he sought to reform students' scholarly interests, identity, and imagination. He was, for example, very careful in his letters to the curriculum committee to emphasize how his courses on the study of "Mexico, Mexican-Americans and Chicano history and culture [were designed to] complicate, not displace, intellectual inquiry," making it clear that his courses were open, as he recalls in an interview with José Antonio Burciaga, "to as many students as are interested" (November 28, 1990). Islas's practice of focusing on Chicano/a literature and yet not directing his teaching exclusively to Chicanos/as made him one of the university's most popular professors. His seminars were always filled to capacity and his lectures drew audiences of over three hundred students. Islas's successfully inclusive and nuanced pedagogical practice not only played a role in his promotion to full professor in 1986, but also led to his renown on the campus for drawing the largest audiences in the humanities.

Part of Islas's ability to successfully speak to a large range of students emerged from his early training as a graduate student in the early 1960s. Yvor Winters had a particularly significant influence on his pedagogy. In this and many other ways, Islas was a Wintersian disciple. Under Winters, Islas developed a passion for language and image. In a lecture titled "The Erotic in Modern Literature," for example, Islas analyzes Nabokov's twenty-three uses of the letter L in the opening two paragraphs of *Lolita*, concluding,

> You may not have been aware of it, but the sound of the letter L will never be the same again for you. Writers have no slides, no visual aids, to show you. They try to create them in your imagination. So they use every trick in the language to seduce your imagination, not your body. Nabokov did not choose the name Lolita by accident. He knows that some of the most sensual words in English . . . have the "l" sound in them: loveliness, delicious, alluring, languish, lascivious, ululate, linger , lustful, lick, etc. (Nabokov's *Lolita* lecture, box 25, folder 9)

As he said in his introductory lecture on *The Portrait of a Lady, Anna Karenina, One Hundred Years of Solitude*, and *Cheri*, to read literature is "to move 'through' books, not 'around' them.—Works have to be read (worse luck, for it takes a long time); it is the only way of discovering what they contain" (Four great novels lecture; box 23, folder 9). In true belletristic tradition, Islas had no qualms about identifying those he considered to be great writers; these included Vargas Llosa, García Márquez, Tolstoy, and Henry James. In a lecture on James, for example, he said he loves

> the work of Henry James, though some of it, particularly in his late and great period, frustrates me no end. The frustration with his later work comes from my being unable to exist in such a rarefied atmosphere with him for as long as he wants me to; I simply cannot breathe in all that ambiguity and not hunger for oxygen or at least a sentence here and there that will help clear up the mist he creates between characters and their intricate relationships to each other. But with James I know that I am in the hands of a true master of writing so that even if I don't comprehend what he is doing or comprehend it just enough to become impatient with it, I'm willing to give him the benefit of my doubts and call him a genius. (Henry James lecture; box 24, folder 8)

Like Winters, Islas was also impatient with writers who were sloppy in diction and thought. Islas thus celebrated writers like Sherwood Anderson, whose writing, he comments in his lecture notes, is "not cluttered like Lewis' and contains the sexuality Cather so scrupulously avoided" (box 22, folder 4). And when it came to his students, he was, like Winters, judgmental. Islas was very leery of jargon in his students' prose, responding to one student: "Thank you for writing in a style relatively free from oppressing jargon, for being in this class, for thinking seriously about these issues." Like Winters, Islas imparted to his students a strong sense of responsibility toward the act of writing. If a student wrote on a poet or a novelist that he or she did not agree with or enjoy, for example, then the student was deceiving himself or herself. To write about literature seriously, Islas believed that you had to be won over completely by the text. For Islas, literature functioned both on an aesthetic level and on a more general level that conveyed a belief or value system. Simply theorizing the text was not good enough for Islas. You had to believe in what the text was doing. Like his mentor Winters, he believed, too, that one had to be moved by the text in order to write about it effectively. Like Winters, then, Islas had little use for theory; accordingly, among literature's many functions was to bring meaning to life. He would open his students' eyes to the nuances of language and technique and to larger meaning in all of his literature courses. His lectures on José Antonio Villarreal's *Pocho* were just as attuned to language as his lectures on Fitzgerald—all the while infusing into both readings dimensions of class, gender, and race. In his notes on his "Masterpieces of American Literature" lecture series, he writes how he wants to take the course only in "directions, themes, concerns I am interested in: Art as social document (i.e. relevant) as aesthetic pleasure." He then asks "how I as a Chicano view literature written by white males: Women, Blacks, Brown, Yellows, Reds" (box 28, folder 10). When Islas lectured to his students on Fitzgerald's *This Side of Paradise,* he began with his own initial dislike of it: "When I first read this book, I was bothered by its superficiality, its inability to come to grips with or linger over what I consider to be the serious in life: real loving as opposed to romantic love; commitment to worthy ideas during one's education; the relationship of the self to the world" (box 23, folder 12). However, after thus identifying himself as an outsider, he deftly moved his students into the novel, showing them how Fitzgerald could appeal in it not just to Chicanos/as but also to those living in a different era.

Islas felt strongly that he had to train his students to read both at the aesthetic and contextual levels. For Islas, the contextual level included not just identification of the historical and social contours of the text, but also a consideration of its reach into the metaphysical. In a lecture on Emily Dickinson's poems he tells his students,

> The human observer is left with the sense of loss and exclusion from that naturalness, that ideal. There is no anguish in this loss; only melancholy. The mystery of death is not lurking here; there is an acceptance of the inevitable. The speaker puts aside her yearning to be a part of nature; she accepts her humanity with no more insight than a slight regret for its limitations. It is one of the moments of greatness in her poetry. You see, she is saying, man can be a most unnatural creature and that is his flaw and his glory. I can only watch the seasons pass; I can only bear the weight of emotions for so long. I can, however, write poetry about this separation between me and nature, between me and immortality, between me and loss or grief or death. And she did. The price in her case was a life of isolation and a private art. She took her work seriously. And *that* is the greatest compliment I pay any writer. (Emily Dickinson lecture; box 22, folder 17)

Likewise, by training students to appreciate the aesthetic and contextual levels in Chicano/a fiction, he sought to avoid tokenizing it—applauding a work simply because it was written by a Chicano/a. For example, when lecturing on Ernesto Galarza's *Education of a Barrio Boy,* he describes it as a "straightforward, unsubtle account of the first 12 yrs. of Galarza's life [that fails to give] us a glimpse into his soul, the inner self that auto-bio should portray" (box 23, folder 7). Those novels that Islas thought worthy of praise were lauded irrespective of ethnic content. He applauds Ron Arias's *The Road to Tamazunchale,* identifying it as the "best written, most carefully wrought and ambitiously conceived, least self-conscious piece of writing available" (book review; box 22, folder 5).

His Wintersian technique of expanding a given close reading out into the world around him led him to create bridges between the world of the text and that of the students. He begins a lecture on Stephen Crane's *The Red Badge of Courage* thus:

> In our day, an appropriate analogy of the kind of change occurring in his lifetime would be the computer "revolution." You are children of the computer era, an era which will change at least in technological ways the way humanity looks at itself. Though it stores the Past, the computer seems more a construct of the Present and the Future. (box 22, folder 16)

Islas would also expand the world of the text by including references to his own personal experiences. For example, in a lecture on Hemingway, Islas strategically adds autobiographical insight into his more traditional literary readings to enliven—and politicize—traditional interpretations and complicate stereotypes. He tells his undergraduates that "working class people of Mexican heritage born and educated in this country" were as much influenced by mainstream popular culture as the next, remarking that his mother read books such as Hemingway's *For Whom the Bell Tolls,* Margaret Mitchell's *Gone with the Wind,* and Fitzgerald's *This Side of Paradise,* enjoying vicariously "all the partying and drinking and running around in limousines. 'I loved to dance all those dances,' she said" (Hemingway and Fitzgerald lecture; box 23, folder 12).[3]

Like Winters, Islas organized his lectures in a systematic and rigid way, providing close readings and also requiring that the students figure out how a given novel fit into the respective culture's values and ideas. (Both men wrote out their lectures completely.) Winters and Islas believed that their approach would provide a way for their students to discover new, creative interpretive readings stemming from their own intellectual identities, separate from the ideas of the professor. Both pushed their students hard to think about why they were reading and what they expected to get out of their reading. (This was very unusual in Winters's day, and still somewhat unusual when Islas began teaching in the early 1970s, when many of his older colleagues still taught literature through a New Critical, decontextualized lens.) At the end of one of the first courses Islas taught as an assistant professor at Stanford, entitled "Masterpieces of American Literature," he concludes the semester asking his students why they should read novels. Is it an escape, he asks, "from the responsibilities of the 'real' world?" Reading good novels, as he reminds students in this same lecture, requires work. Reading novels in his course was not about comfortably absorbing narratives that only spoke to the student's experiences. He wanted them to get more out of the readings. Working hard at interpreting good narrative fiction and poetry, in Islas's mind, expanded the readers' vision of the world to see new ways of existing, beyond the self. For Islas, then, fiction could use a "descriptive" (distinguishing it from a "prescriptive") realism to detail worlds that resonate directly with the reader's reality outside the text and to "tell us something about this corner or that corner of the prison":

> Novels extract from the "real" world in order to compose worlds of their own. The novel does not attempt to give all the facts but the pattern of some of them. And no matter how "objective" in method, the novel always has a stance. A special kind of mind is at work—one that is sensitive to the overtones of facts and to the overtones of people and to music they make when they combine. The novelist's comments on the history of human beings are always, in the highest sense, biased. This biased stance is what I suspect you to be thinking about when you ask a book to give you a message, to give you a prescription for your day-to-day life. For shame! (English literature lecture; box 28, folder 11)

However, as he is careful to remind his students, "Like all art, the novel's obligation to reality as I suspect you see it, is obscure. It can therefore be

more real than real. The novel can also make the unimaginative imag-
ine—imagination" (box 28, folder 11). He concludes the lecture, "There.
That's all there is. We've dealt with fictions, illusions, mysteries all quar-
ter. If at any time you felt or sensed or comprehended their *reality,* then
you got the essential elements out of this course. And I did my job. If you
didn't, try again."

Islas also shared with Winters a style of interacting with students that
was persistent, brusque, irreverent, and sarcastic; but, like Winters, Islas
could also be generous and good-humored, if he felt the student deserved
it.[4] Also like Winters, Islas was revered by the students he mentored.[5]
Other students saw Islas as a pugnacious antagonist. Winters and Islas
generally preferred lecturing from a podium—believing in the need to
make patent the hierarchy separating the student from the professor—
and both would lecture liberally on their own works. Both saw themselves
as performers who aimed to provoke and impassion their students.

That Yvor Winters had a strong and enduring influence on Islas's
teaching style and pedagogic worldview is more than clear. This worked
as a strong guide to Islas, who evolved into a great teacher and who
showed an enthusiasm for and profound knowledge of all types of liter-
ature within their larger social, political, and historical contexts. With this
pedagogical framework, he was able to realize his goal of creating an at-
mosphere of reciprocity between Anglo and Other canons that would
eventually lead, as he writes about his popular "Masterpieces of Ameri-
can Literature" course, to "a cross-canonization in the academy" (box 26,
folder 1). In 1988, he recalled to a lecture hall filled with students the time
when he took the course in 1957,

> when the American literature we have read together this quarter [Twain,
> Whitman, Melville, James, O'Connor, Cather] was seen as the "minority"
> literature. Now, these very same writers and works are seen by some as
> part of a "canon." I trust and hope that what is called "minority" literature
> or literature written by feminist women now will, too, have future canons
> of their own. And that eventually, there will be cross-canonization in the
> academy. Looking at the treasure of Afro-American literature now being
> unearthed and made available, at the territory that Native American,
> Asian American and Hispanic American writers women and men are ex-
> ploring in their worthy desire to have their respective people's contribu-

tions to the history and life of what we call North America known and appreciated, I see an exciting world of fictions opening up and out. It's very much the kind of excitement we young student majors in the mid-50s felt being in a course offered for the very first time and called Masterpieces of American Literature. (box 26, folder 1)

Islas did not want to undermine existing canons; he wanted to reform and rebuild them. For Islas, good critics and writers take the "time and energy to read carefully" and "never play it safe"; they craft essays and narrative fiction to open readers' eyes and jar them out of any "national complacency they might feel" (box 26, folder 1). He was thrilled to see his novel *The Rain God* appear on the list of required novels for the newly revised "Culture, Ideas, and Values" course in 1988, reading it as a sign that he had attained his goal of cross-pollinating the noncanonical with the canonical to help transform the topography of the American literary canon.

Islas's rebuilding of the master's house took place not just in courses where he introduced Chicano/a authors (including himself), but in his literature courses generally. In American literature courses he would have students read and study James Baldwin and Richard Wright alongside Faulkner, Melville, or Twain, and, as they became available, Zora Neale Hurston, Toni Morrison, Maxine Hong Kingston, and Cherríe Moraga. In a lecture on Wright, for example, he announces, "No writer before Crane in North American letters had taken a serious look at the wretchedness of the poor from a clinical rather than a sentimental perspective. It seems tame to us now by comparison to novels since then which have treated poverty and violence (inner and outer) artfully and to even greater effect than Crane. Wright's *Native Son* and *Black Boy* come to mind" (box 22, folder 16). And in a course that focused on more the canonical Anglo-American writers Fitzgerald and Hemingway, he would ask his students to "look at these characters and their pre-occupations from a lower middle class ethnic perspective" (Hemingway and Fitzgerald lecture; box 23, folder 12).

Islas conceived and taught American literature as multiculturally inclusive, lecturing on both canonical and noncanonical authors within the same analytic frame, with the goal of reshaping the students' imaginative (social, racial, sexual) expectations. He aimed to enrich his students' sense of the "the exciting world of fictions" within a complex spectrum of race, gender, and class that explodes, he announces in another lecture, "old textual conceptions of what it means to participate in the history and life of what we call North America" (Masterpieces of American literature lecture; box 26, folder 1). For example, in a two-day lecture series on E. M. Forster's *Maurice* that Islas gave in 1975—a time in the academy when queer readings in literature were largely taboo—he announces to his students,

> Up until four or five years ago, if anyone had told me that I would be lecturing about male homosexuality to [a] group of Stanford students in a course that offered five units of credit, I would not have believed them. . . . I do not intend to be condescending or to prescribe behavior that is still considered worse than murder by a large segment of our society. I hope instead to walk the middle way and describe to you what I know about this subject as it relates to literature. (box 23, folder 6)

In this controversial course, Islas lectured on Forster's great success at "portraying homosexual love" in his defiance of post-Victorian conventions holding that "all sexual *mis*behavior must be punished in life and literature" (box 23, folder 6). The posthumously published *Maurice*, he told his students, broke the "necessary and hard ground for future writers of any sex who wish to cultivate the territory of homosexual love" (box 23, folder 6). He also lectured on gay novelists James Baldwin and Gore Vidal. Both writers, he said, "ultimately fail in their attempts to portray love between males in their fiction. They fall into to two large traps common to writers who place themselves self-consciously within minority groups. For Homosexual writers, one of those traps is Champion for a Sexual Cause and the other is the trap of Punishment and Guilt" (E. M. Forster lecture; box 23, folder 6). Islas criticizes Vidal for being a "Champion for a Sexual Cause"; to say

> that only homosexuals can have worthy and equal relationships because they are not caught up in the role playing that goes on between men and women is as wrong as saying that only heterosexuals can have worthy relationships because their union will produce children. One asks the heterosexuals: what about childless marriages? broken homes? illegitimate

children, and so on? One asks the homosexuals: what about the role play-
ing that goes on between the more or less effeminate or masculine part-
ners of those relationships? (E. M. Forster lecture)

Islas admired Baldwin, but was critical of his *Go Tell It on the Mountain*
and *Giovanni's Room*—novels he felt revealed a "writer who is self-
consciously homosexual" and trapped in feeling either the need to be
punished or intense guilt. He tells his students, "One or both of the male
characters who have slept together in these books must suffer and suffer
and suffer. One or both of them must be killed off. And this must happen
to them because of sex, not because of character. And if they don't suffer
punishment they must inflict it on others" (box 23, folder 6). Finally, ac-
cording to Islas, in these two novels Baldwin "sees fit to kill off one of his
lovers and put the other back in his closet" (box 23, folder 6). Islas thought
Another Country did a better job at portraying a complex queer relation-
ship, but he was critical of its lack of "female/female sexual relationships"
(box 23, folder 6). Islas identified this as not just as a trait of Baldwin's, but
something symptomatic of a culture at large that is either unwilling, he
tells his students, "to explore deeply the erotic relationships between
women" or that only describes female-female desire as "sick" or as
"pornographic devices to arouse the male" (box 23, folder 6). Baldwin of-
fers two main lessons, Islas concludes: "the first is that there can be no se-
rious erotic relationship between women; and the second is that once a
woman finds a good man to show her what it's really all about, she will
remain exclusively his and heterosexual" (box 23, folder 6).

While Islas attended to specific gay/lesbian themes and characteriza-
tions, he was also attuned to issues of gender and sexuality generally. For
example, in the course "The Erotic in Modern Literature," which he gave
in 1979, he notes the tendency of male authors such as Vladimir Nabokov,
Marcel Proust, and Philip Roth to equate virility with the notion of man-
hood. Islas addresses candidly the issue of the phallus in literature:

> The male anatomy lends itself to such an equation. From the very begin-
> ning of male sexual awareness, the penis, in its wonderful capacity to
> grow and shrink as if *with a will of its own*, can often or at least more than
> occasionally be beyond the control of one's character or sensibility or even
> desire. The male, then, learns to attribute to his penis a personality or even

a character of its own that does not care about what other people or even [what] the man himself thinks. Everyone in this room who has a penis knows from long experience exactly what I am talking about. Now a male identifies himself with the unpredictable behavior of his penis, he is identifying sex with character. It is more complicated than this oversimplification suggests, especially when we consider this society's demands on males to behave in certain ways sexually, but let's leave it at that. Philip Roth in *Portnoy's Complaint* (by the way is in the *locked* stacks of the Main Library) has portrayed the behavior of the penis in order to draw his portrait of a man who cannot join society. Alexander Portnoy's obsession with his male member keeps him removed from society and Roth, through this metaphor of Portnoy's obsession, creates one of the best comic characters in Modern American fiction. (The erotic in modern literature lecture; box 22, folder 20)

In another course on American literature, Islas moved into more general discussions of North American mainstream culture and its Puritanical backbone. Such a culture, according to Islas, makes synonymous "God, patriotism and heterosexuality" and enforces this with a legal system that, ironically, incarcerates and seeks to rehabilitate men caught performing "unnatural acts" by putting them in a place "surrounded by only men and where such behavior will naturally continue. The hypocrisy is overwhelming" (box 23, folder 6). And in a lecture given in this course on Hawthorne and Melville, he elaborates on how this Puritanism informs a restrictive vision of characters gendered either male or female. Such writers, according to Islas, reductively ascribe "femininity to those who are artistic, and masculinity to those who are intellectual" (box 22, folder 1). As a result, these writers get themselves into the kind of trouble Henry James avoided through his use, according to Islas, of a "comic approach to the dichotomy" (box 22, folder 1). While Islas read certain North American writers who gendered their characters (restrictively or not) within a puritanist ideology, he also lectured on the masculine/feminine duality, complicated by the role of the family, in Latin American fiction. In a lecture on García Márquez's *One Hundred Years of Solitude,* he comments,

> that for all its mythical extravagance and magic, the book is rooted in conventional notions about the roles of men and women in the world. . . .

THE FAMILY and one's role as man or woman with respect to the family are the important facts of life. One's individuality must be sacrificed to the family. Only THE FAMILY guarantees the continuance of life. Only if one fulfills one's duty as male or female to the idea of THE FAMILY can civilization above all as we know it go on. . . . That the Buendías have the mark of solitude does not mean they are individuals. It means they are alienated, set apart, existentially different from the other families in Macondo. (box 23, folder 8)

Islas shows that Latin American writers, unlike their North American counterparts, subordinate gender dichotomies to the family. This is not to say that such writers do not dichotomize to a destructive degree. However, just as Islas found that Henry James's approach to female/male gendering could be redeemed by its comic aspects, so too does he rescue García Márquez by identifying his use of parody in his characterization of the "roles that men and women are given to play in this world" (box 23, folder 8).

As a Chicano scholar and professor, Islas was careful not to subscribe to categories that he believed would essentialize racial, gendered, sexual, and class identity and experience. As he announced at one point late in his career to a hall filled with California State University teachers, "I agree with Eudora Welty when she tells us that's what writers do: restore illusions. What teachers do is to display those illusions to their students" (box 23, folder 12). Islas was weary of the overly politicized rhetoric and posturing among queer, lesbian, feminist, and Chicano/a writers, which seemed to simplify subjectivity. At the same time that he was critical of such writers and their often essentialist and simplistic characterizations, he was also sympathetic to the anger of these writers. While Islas understood the value of essentialism—for instance, it served to make dramatically visible an otherwise invisible community's experience with oppression—he ultimately saw sexuality, gender, and race as informed by a complex array of experiences and possible self-expressions inspired and not restricted by the past, the community, and the family. For Islas, as he told Antonio Burciaga, to be queer and Chicano was to be able to "create oneself continually."

CODA "A Dancing with Ghosts"

Dancing with Ghosts focuses on the prismatic conjunctions and disjunctions that informed Arturo Islas's life, his aesthetic ambitions, and his poetic achievements. As a Chicano (simultaneously American and Mexican), he was determined to interweave the Chicano literary tradition with what he considered the best works within the world literary corpus, mainly in terms of narrative techniques and the care in the crafting of both prose and poetry. At the same time, Islas was a deeply conflicted man who at times internalized the racism and homophobia he abhorred. He showed a confident face to the world that masked deep insecurities about himself as an imperfect being. Ears, limp, scat bag—all these he sometimes experienced as outward manifestations of an ineradicable inner imperfection. The vibrant and intricately choreographed movements that appear in Islas's fiction, poetry—and engagement with the world generally—poignantly reveal his attempt to reconcile the divisions and contrasts he experienced as a Chicano growing up on the U.S./Mexico border and later as a gay man living in the San Francisco Bay Area. Perhaps, as the biography suggests and as Islas himself imagined, reconciliation, for Islas, could take place only in that space in between a present filled with ghosts from the past and a past vividly alive with figures from the present; in that space in between growing up in the life-filled southwestern desert and maturing in the death-filled San Francisco Bay Area. In the final instance, his reconciliation takes place in that mental and social space where he learns to deal with the fact that his life is a dance with a myriad of ghosts: his father, whose emotional distance and rigid machismo were sources of great pain; his mother, whose plaintive acceptance of her subordination stirred him to anger; his paternal grandmother, who bequeathed to him both a love for literature and a kernel of self-loathing as *indio;* his uncle Carlos, closeted, murdered in his hometown; Jay Spears, whom he loved. Islas's reconciliation—his dancing with ghosts—is his way of being in the world and inventing a hybrid narrative and poetic aesthetics where fact and fiction touch, twirl, and collapse into one organic whole. Islas expressed his sense of identity and experience as an in-between space involving an irreducible mixture of worlds.

I take the title of the biography from a poem Islas wrote in 1978, "Dancing with Ghosts," where he artfully expresses his sense of finding a place in the world in between a vast array of contradictory sexual, racial, physical, and social experiences (box 9, folder 11). In this nine-part poem, Islas invents a poet-narrator that moves back and forth between the El Paso desert (warm memories of childhood, home, and dramatic desertscapes) and San Francisco (painful meditations on feelings of isolation as an adult in an alienating urbanscape). The voice shifts from that of a calm and soothing tone to one filled with anger and bitterness; it shifts from recollecting a sense of belonging in the El Paso of his past— memories of "vitex trees and greasewood after rain" delight his senses— to a present in San Francisco filled with despondency, pain, and suffering. It is at this moment when the poet-narrator describes his alcohol binges—"a dancing with ghosts as I hold onto a drink / For dumb, dear life"—his unrequited love, and the S&M encounters where bodies grope "for a soul." Ultimately, however, Islas's poet-narrator comes to terms with his life by embracing his many "ghosts gazing at the foothills," for it is those ghosts that, paradoxically, allow him to let go of the memories of his long lost love. In the final part of the poem, Islas's poet-narrator finds a sense of self-affirmation. He states:

> Look on me as a brother in the desert,
> More than a survivor delivered from phantoms,
> Who sees in the crimson reflections of the mountain,
> In the freesias falling over these wastes,
> An eagerness, a readiness, to love himself.

In his writing, Islas brings to life his many coexisting selves (factual and fictional) and reverses, complicates, and undermines those dichotomies (El Paso versus Palo Alto, Palo Alto versus San Francisco, desert versus ocean, Chicano versus Anglo, mind versus body, past versus present) that would otherwise have regulated and controlled his identity and experience. Islas danced with his ghosts in life, narrative, and poetry to embrace and celebrate the possibility of experiencing new ways of existing in the world.

Islas left a world much remade by his presence precisely because he had the courage and the skill to dance with his inherited world—real and ghostly—and give it an artistic expression. Like the complex root-webs of the desert plants of his childhood, he absorbed as much of life as he could while he struggled to endure, grow, and transform himself and the literary landscape of his time. His spirit has eloquently survived his death—through his fiction, his poetry, and his legacy as a teacher.

Chronology of Major Events

1938	On May 25, Arturo Islas La Farga was born in El Paso, Texas; he spent his early childhood in the Five Points Area, a few blocks from El Paso's El Segundo Barrio.
1946	In the last week of September, Islas was diagnosed with the polio that would eventually result in a limp.
1951–56	Islas attended El Paso High School—the school his parents and *tías* and *tíos* had attended—and graduated valedictorian.
1956	Islas entered Stanford as an undergraduate with an Alfred P. Sloan scholarship.
1957	In the fall, Islas's craft as a short story writer won him acceptance into a graduate creative writing class with Hortense Callisher.

1959	José Antonio Villarreal published *Pocho* with New York's Doubleday—a novel that Islas later critiqued for being a sentimental, essentializing portrait of Chicano subjectivity.
1960	Islas graduated with a BA in English (minor in religious studies) in June and then entered the Stanford English department as a PhD candidate in the fall.
	Islas enrolled in Yvor Winters's "Chief American Poets," which would shape his critical worldview and poetic sensibility.
1962	In the spring quarter, Islas enrolled in another influential course, Wallace Stegner's "Development of the Short Story."
1967	The night of February 19, Islas's Uncle Carlos was murdered by an eighteen-year-old Anglo soldier he had allegedly picked up in a bar on the south side of El Paso. Islas spiraled into deep depression.
	Disenchanted with academics, Islas took time off from the PhD program just before beginning to write his dissertation.
	During his time off, Islas had many jobs, including one working as a speech therapist at the V.A. hospital in Menlo Park—the same hospital where Ken Kesey, author of *One Flew over the Cuckoo's Nest* (1973), had worked in 1959.
1969	Stanford professor Ian Watt convinced Islas to finish his PhD.
	Islas returned to Stanford in January 1969 to write his dissertation—"The Work of Hortense Callisher: On Middle Ground."
	In June, Islas underwent a colostomy at Stanford Medical.
1971	Islas completed his dissertation on Hortense Callisher and was hired by Stanford as a tenure-track professor in the English department.
	Islas, Renato Rosaldo, Jerry Porras, and Jim Leckie established the Chicano Fellows Program to address the needs of Chicano/a faculty and students at Stanford.
	Islas taught the first Chicano literature course ("Chicano Themes") at Stanford.
1972	Islas became seriously involved with Jay Spears, who was an inspiring force behind his fiction writing; he appears as the character Virgil Spears in *La Mollie and the King of Tears* and the character Sam Godwin in *Migrant Souls*.
1973	Islas began to explore the S&M and bathhouse scene in San Francisco.
1976	In March, Islas was promoted to associate professor on the basis of a draft of his novel, *Día de los muertos* (an early version of *The Rain God*), as well as on the basis of his teaching.

1977	In the fall, Islas began his sabbatical year off; he rewrote *Día de los muertos* and wrote poetry.
1984–85	Islas helped to revamp the "Western Civilization" requirement by including works by women and minority writers.
1984	In October, Islas's *The Rain God* was published with the Palo Alto–based Alexandrian Press.
1985	The *Los Angeles Times* nominated *The Rain God* for its best fiction award.
1986	On January 25, *The Rain God* won the Southwest Book Award for its literary excellence and enrichment of the cultural heritage of the Southwest and Islas was promoted to full professor. While a visiting professor at the University of Texas-El Paso, Islas taught "Creative Writing for Bilingual Students" and began to draft his novel *La Mollie and the King of Tears*.
1987	Islas continued working on *La Mollie* and received an advance contract to write a sequel to *The Rain God*.
1988	On January 14, Islas learned that he had tested positive test for HIV antigens.
1991	On February 15, Arturo Islas died of pneumonia at his home on the Stanford University campus. Just before his death, the University of Texas-El Paso elected him to its Writers Hall of Fame.

Notes

INTRODUCTION

1.   Journal citations that include box and folder information are from the Arturo Islas Papers; journal citations not including such information are from Paul Skenazy's collection of journal entries.

CHAPTER ONE

1.   In *Latinos: A Biography of the People,* Earl Shorris critiques Arturo Islas Jr.'s representation in *The Rain God* of the father as a "crude man, a tough cop who is unable to understand an intellectually curious, physically weak son." Shorris, of the same generation as Arturo Sr., felt that Arturo Islas Sr. was a figure who had

shown a "gentleness" toward those he had arrested and who was full of "pride" toward his son (434). For Shorris, *The Rain God* is a "novel of exorcism, an attempt to get rid of his own devils" (435) that misrepresents machismo. As far as Shorris is concerned, the *macho* is a figure who can maintain dignity in the face of adversity and who takes responsibility for his actions. For Shorris, Arturo Islas Sr. is the apotheosis of the *macho* (his "sense of order, of the moderating role of civilization") whose courageous acts have had some lasting, positive effect in the world (437).

2.   Islas fictionalizes this early experience in grade school in his short story "Poor Little Lamb." Here, he invents the character Miguel, "Mike," to fictionalize this early estrangement, writing, "The first years of his education were spent in loneliness and fear. An intelligent student, he would nevertheless sneak into the closet of the first grade classroom and cry, overwhelmed with a longing for his mother and a terrible fear of whether he would be able to do his lessons correctly on the following day" (Aldama 2003, 20).

CHAPTER TWO

1.   All the short stories, poetry, and academic texts discussed in this chapter appear in Aldama (2003).

2.   As noted earlier, Islas was also frustrated in his attempts to publish his 1975 monograph, "Saints, Artists, and Vile Politics."

3.   In *Dialectics of Our Americas*, José David Saldívar (1991) nicely sums up the objective of Víctor Villaseñor's *Macho!* and José Antonio Villarreal's *Pocho*: they were written "according to New York editors' standards about certain U.S. ethnic themes—social maladjustment, the individual and his environment, the pathological character of the Chicano family, Illegals, violence, and criminal behavior" (112).

4.   Many of the other essays that have since been written on *The Rain God* are published in my edited collection, *Critical Mappings of Arturo Islas's Fictions* (Bilingual Review/Press): John Honerkamp's "Awash in a Valley of Tears: The Dialectics of Generation in Arturo Islas's *The Rain God*"; Vivian Nun Halloran's "The Monstrous Pseudo-Pregnant Body as Border-Crossing Metaphor in *The Rain God*"; David N. Ybarra's "Another Closet in the House of Angels: The Denial of a Homosexual Identity in *The Rain God*"; Karen E. H. Skinazi's "Out of Personhood, Out of Print: Cultural Censorship from Harriet Wilson to Arturo Islas"; David Rice's "Sinners among Angels or Family History and the Ethnic Narrator in Arturo Islas's *The Rain God* and *Migrant Souls*"; Theresa Meléndez's "*El Contrabando de El Paso*: Islas and Geographies of Knowing"; Michael Hardin's "Make a Run from the Borderlands: Arturo Islas's *The Rain God* and *Migrant Souls* and the

Need to Escape Homophobic Masternarratives"; Rosemary Weatherston's "The Creative Deformation That Is Plot': Arturo Islas, Cultural Authenticity, and Ethno/biography"; and Mimi Gladstein's "From El Paso to Del Sapo: Intersections of Biography and Fiction."

5.   *The Rain God* continued to receive great reviews and tremendous scholarly appreciation. However, it also upset some family members, who felt that family secrets had been betrayed. Islas's cousin Patty cut off all communication with Islas after publication of the novel, which fictionalized the violent murder of her closeted gay father, Carlos ("Felix" in the novel). In the sequel, *Migrant Souls,* Islas deliberately thematized this confusion of the "real" as it is presented in the fictional narrative with the real of the world out there. Josie says sarcastically, "You have to stop writing about our perfectly happy family. . . . The older generation does not approve. They think you're telling their terrible secrets to the world and they don't like it" (209). Islas's immediate family also read *The Rain God* as more autobiographical (referential) than fictional, but did not object.

6.   The initial resistance by publishers may have stemmed in part from the fact that such a borderland fiction had yet to be recognized as a viable creative response to everyday reality in the United States. Gloria Anzaldúa's *Borderland/La Frontera* was published in 1987 by a small publisher, Aunt Lute.

7.   Islas followed the life of James Baldwin closely, collecting many news clippings by and/or about Baldwin. Islas was particularly touched by an essay ("Breaks a Silence") wherein Baldwin said of the "American artist," "I know exactly what Nathaniel Hawthorne meant when he wrote, from England, around 1861, that 'the United States may be fit for many excellent purposes, but they are not fit to live in.' Nearly all American artists have felt this, and for very good reason" (box 22, folder 7). Later, Islas would express his own mixed feelings about being an "American artist," remarking on the "old fear of being dismissed for being gay because now more than ever hatred-and-fear of gays runs rampant in the land" (journal, February 10, 1987; box 2, folder 1). This fear led to paralyzing anxieties and deeply entrenched writing blocks.

8.   Islas was also a perfectionist when it came to dress and social manners, a perfectionism that he cultivated from an early age to hide deep insecurities brought on by his postpolio limp and his father's denigration.

9.   Islas divided writers into two categories: those like Norman Mailer, who fail to transform personal experience into something larger than the self (he saw Mailer as "too-ego-concerned, too in love with his own main preoccupation: the glory of Norman Mailer"), and those like Emily Dickinson, who can transform the deeply personal into the universal.

10.   See also Mimi Gladstein's autobiographically informed essay, "From El Paso to Del Sapo: Intersections of Biography and Fiction" (collected in *Critical Mappings of Arturo Islas's Fictions),* which explores Islas's blurring of the bound-

aries between biographical fact and narrative fiction in *La Mollie and the King of Tears* in order to make room for the texturing of his many characters and selves.

11.   Islas was influenced not only by Yvor Winters's poetics, but also by his approach to critically evaluating literature. When Islas wrote his dissertation and later began to teach at Stanford, he would use Winters's "assertively evaluative" critical approach when discussing and analyzing literature. In this spirit, for narrative fiction and poetry to be "good," it had to appeal to aspects of the reader's intellect as well to all his or her senses; it had to reintegrate the reader's spirit. Winters also had a significant influence on Islas's pedagogical method and style. I discuss Winters's influence on Islas as a scholar and teacher at length in chapter 5. Islas's affinity for Winters (also known by those close to him as "Arthur") was more than simply literary. Both had had close brushes with death, Winters with tuberculosis as a young man and Islas with polio and later an ulcerated colon.

12.   Notably, while Islas eventually turned away from exploring his borderland Chicano/a poetics, one of his graduate students, Francisco X. Alarcón, picked up where he left off and is now a major gay Chicano poet. Alarcón invents poetic speakers who move between multiple discursive and spatial forms of racial and sexual being.

13.   In "Desire," Islas alludes to lesbian poet Elizabeth Bishop's *Geography III.* Bishop, too, was interested in how a series of poetic lines can form boxes/rooms that suggest only partial views into contained worlds. Perhaps as a consequence of her closeted lesbian identity, she used the poem to both reveal and obscure.

14.   Islas continued to develop this *rasquache* poetics in the 1980s. In a poem that he read at the Chicano Literary Criticism in a Social Context National Conference at Stanford, May 28–30, 1987, he hybridized language to call attention to racial hierarchies of difference that continue to exist (box 29, folder 5):

"BETWEEN THE SHEETS [CHITS]" FOR LORNA DEE CERVANTES
WITH A NOD TOWARD T. S. ELIOT

> Between the page y la palabra
>   falls the writer
> Between el editor and the publisher
>   falls the writer
> Between el criticón and the reader
>   falls the writer
> Between the discourse and the praxis
>   falls the writer
> Between the story y la Historia
>   falls the writer
> Between la persona and the people
>   falls the writer
> Between la idea and the art
>   falls the writer
> Between el cielo and the earth
>   falls the writer

A veces demanding
De vez-en-cuando comanding
Pero nunca, nunca contento
with landing.
¿Ya se cayó?
¿Quién? ¿el escritor o la escritora?
Pues esos que nomás saben palabras.
    No. No se quieren callar

CHAPTER THREE

1. Islas was delighted by this sociosexual transformation, the effects of which could be seen in new trends in literature. In 1964, the Supreme Court decided to clear the way for Grove Press to republish Henry Miller's controversial *Tropic of Cancer*. Grove subsequently published a series of queer-themed titles such as Jean Genet's *Our Lady of the Flowers*, Burroughs's *Naked Lunch*, and John Rechy's *City of Night*. Islas's favorite author, James Baldwin, hit the best-seller list with *Another Country*. These works did not characterize gay figures as one-dimensional, diseased, or as criminally outlawed cardboard cutouts. Queer desire was also finding its way into the novels and poems coming out of San Francisco's North Beach. Islas followed closely the work of Beats like Robert Duncan, Jack Spicer, and Robin Blaser. Islas especially enjoyed the way Allen Ginsberg's "Howl" turned the tables on stereotypes by giving voice to a positively celebrated queer erotic.

2. Islas was disturbed by the obituary that appeared in the *San Francisco Chronicle*. He was upset that the newspaper failed to include information about Jay's personal life, instead focusing exclusively on his work as an attorney.

3. Islas still did not feel like he could turn to the Chicano community for support, harboring a deep fear of coming out to Chicanos/as. On one occasion, during a Chicano/a studies conference at Stanford in the spring of 1987 (its proceedings and papers were published as the groundbreaking *Criticism in the Borderlands* in 1991), Islas writes in his journal: "I expect them to destroy me, at least to harm me in some way. I do not feel 'them' to be a source of emotional support. Much of my feeling can be traced to childhood terrors about being Mexican and about Mexicans. How easily, automatically, compulsively, they turn human beings, ideas, etc. into potentially harmful monsters" (May 25, 1987; box 2, folder 1). Islas also had deep conflicts regarding his racial and sexual identification. With a few exceptions, he dated only white men. He was aware of this, often commenting in his journals on his own internalized racism as it intersected with his queer desire. There was the obvious racism that he experienced daily, but there was also the more subtle racism he himself reproduced—the internalized voice of his paternal grandmother, Crecenciana.

CHAPTER FOUR

1.   In helping Islas, Watt was also helping the department. As the depart-ment's first Chicano professor, Watt realized, Islas would be able to help meet the emerging multicultural curricular demands.

2.   When Islas was drinking, he also craved cocaine, but even cocaine no longer helped take the edge off. In a journal entry dated May 13, 1987, he writes how his cocaine habit had abused his "poor nose" and destroyed his sinuses to the point that his "sense of smell had been dulled" and that he suffered from "constant dryness and bloody discharges" (box 2, folder 1).

3.   Though Islas rejected the gay French theorist Michel Foucault's post-structural analysis of history, he sympathized with Foucault's decision to keep his HIV status private. Like Foucault, Islas did not want to be visible as a "per-verse" subject controlled by a homophobic nation-state.

CHAPTER FIVE

1.   As noted in chapter 4, Islas, plagued by abdominal pain, was also drawn to the protection afforded by the health coverage he would have at Stanford.

2.   *El Grito* also had a small press off-shoot it called El Quinto Sol that issued the first Chicano anthology of writing, *El Espejo* (The mirror). El Quinto Sol's ed-itor, Octavio Romano, had published over sixty new Chicano writers by the early 1970s. After a lawsuit crushed El Quinto Sol, Romano opened another publishing venture, Tonatiuh International, the first to publish Rudolfo A. Anaya's *Bless Me, Última,* which became a best-seller.

3.   He brought his personal experience to bear on his discussion of Hem-ingway and Fitzgerald: "In addition to looking at them through the lens of the writer, I also have the privilege of seeing them in relation to my own experience of teaching them at a place like Stanford. I have spent thirty years of my life here, more than half of those years standing on the solitary side of the lectern. The stu-dents have stayed the same age; I am the one who has grown older. I like to think that my own 'growth'—whatever that big word means—in relation to these writ-ers and this university contains something interesting and instructive and that is one reason I continue to offer this course. As I have said on more than one occa-sion: I did not want to teach this course from the beginning and I did so the first time because none of my colleagues in American literature volunteered to do so. They, like me, did not care much for Hemingway. I finally agreed to try if I could include Fitzgerald in the syllabus. And so twelve years ago, this course became a part of our curriculum.

Sixteen years before that, at the beginning of my senior year at Stanford, my parents gave me their '55 Chevrolet and I drove that wonderful car to and from

Stanford and the southwest until the transmission gave out in 1964. Fitzgerald would have loved that car and the things I did in it. Even the colors would have appealed to him: pink and charcoal gray. Gasoline in those days was more expensive than in his time but it was still cheap—eighteen to thirty-three cents a gallon, depending upon gas wars. Tuition at Stanford had just been raised from $250 to $350 a quarter. Those were the good things" (box 23, folder 12).

4.   In one student evaluation, a student marked "excellent" for the instructor's "knowledge of subject" and comments, "be prepared for an instructor whose wit verges on the sarcastic, and has no qualms about nasty remarks to students" (box 26, folder 28).

5.   After a year teaching at the University of Texas-El Paso Islas also gathered a cadre of devoted students. One such student, Tracey, writes him a letter dated March, 1987: "Dear *Dear* Arturo, . . . I do miss your class—the ideas, the arguments, the way your whole face carries your thoughts, carries more than your thoughts. I miss and don't miss meeting with such a sensitively sensual, intelligent person, man, as yourself, once a week, every week. I hope you don't hear this as caca flattery. . . . It's rare being jolted and soothed by the same soul all at once. I *do* miss your class. Love, Tracey" (box 26, folder 10). And another student who took Islas's course on Chicano/a literature in 1990 writes: "The best course of my Stanford experience. Prof. Islas is frank and constructive as well as helpful in his criticism and complementing of all assignments. The most relevant to my personal experience as a Chicana at Stanford!" (box 27, folder 12). And random comments from students evaluating his 1988 course on Fitzgerald and Hemingway read as follows: "A fantastic class—Islas lives up to his reputation"; "Islas is the best professor I've had!"; "wonderful lecturer. good anecdotes"; "It was my favorite class to go to. Excellent lecture—I'll never forget it"; "Great to hear a writer's perspective/opinion and interpretation mixed with context"; "This man is *awesome*; never let him leave!"; "His lectures weave spell of attention-grabbing magic" (box 27, folder 13).

Bibliography

Aguilar Melantzón, Ricardo. 1987. "Torica with Arturo Islas: An Interview." *Nova Quarterly* 22, no. 4:2–4.

Aldama, Frederick Luis. 2000. "Ethnoqueer Re-Architexturing of Metropolitan Space." *Nepantla* 1, no. 3:581–604.

———. 2003. *Arturo Islas: The Uncollected Works.* Houston: Arte Público Press.

———. 2005. *Critical Mappings of Arturo Islas's Fictions.* Tempe: Bilingual Review/Press.

Arturo Islas Papers. Special Collections Library, Stanford University.

Bruce-Novoa, Juan. 1986. "Homosexuality and the Chicano Novel." *Confluencia* 2, no. 1:69–77.

Cantú, Roberto. 1992. *Dictionary of Literary Biography.* 2nd ed. Detroit: Gale Research.

Galindo, Luis Alberto. 1985. "El dios de la lluvia = RAIN GOD." *La Comunidad* 241:12–13.

Gillenkirk, Jeff. 1990. Review of *Migrant Souls. Nation,* March 5, 313–14.

Gladstein, Mimi. 1990. Review of *Migrant Souls. El Paso Times,* March 11, 2D.

Gonzales-Berry, Erlinda. 1985. "Sensuality, Repression, and Death in *The Rain God.*" *Bilingual Review: La Revista Bilingüe* 12, no. 3:258–61.

González, Ray. 1991. "The Migrant Soul of Arturo Islas." *Guadalupe Review* 1:116–23.

———. 1991. "One Great Haiku in a Lifetime: An Interview with Arturo Islas." *Guadalupe Review* 1:124–34.

Goode, Stephen. 1984. Book review of *The Rain God: A Desert Tale. Nuestro* 8, no. 7:48.

Gutierrez Castillo, Dina. 1988. "La imagen de la mujer en la novela fronteriza." In *Mujer y literatura mexicana y chicana: Culturas en contacto,* edited by Aralia López-González, 55–63. Mexico City: Colegio de la Frontera Norte.

Halper, Leah. 1993. "Ofrenda for Arturo Islas." *San Jose Studies* 19, no. 1:62–72.

Islas, Arturo. 1984. *The Rain God: A Desert Tale.* Palo Alto: Alexandrian Press.

———. 1988. "Chakespeare Louie San Francisco 1973." *Zyzzyva* 4, no. 1:79–84.

———. 1990a. INTERVIEW. *Bay Area Reporter* 10, no. 13:3, 29.

———. 1990b. *Migrant Souls.* New York: Avon Books.

———. 1991. "The Politics of Imaginative Writing." In *Critical Fictions,* edited by Philomena Mariani, 72–74. Seattle: Bay Press.

———. 1996. *La Mollie and the King of Tears.* Albuquerque: University of New Mexico Press.

Márquez, C. Antonio. 1994. "The Historical Imagination in Arturo Islas's *The Rain God* and *Migrant Souls.*" *MELUS* 19, no. 2:3–16.

Mayer, Henry. 1990. "An Immigrant Family's Diminished Dreams." *San Francisco Chronicle,* February 18, 3.

McKenna, Teresa. 1997. *Migrant Song: Politics and Process in Contemporary Chicano Literature.* Austin: University of Texas Press.

Middlebrook, Diane Wood. 1996. "Telling Stories." In *The Seduction of Biography,* edited by Mary Rhiel and David Suchoff, 123–29. New York: Routledge.

Ortíz, Ricardo L. 1993. "Sexuality Degree Zero: Pleasure and Power in the Novels of John Rechy, Arturo Islas, and Michael Nava." *Journal of Homosexuality* 26, nos. 2–3:111–27.

Portillo, Febe. 1988. "Syncretism in Counter-hegemonic Literature by Latinos in the United States." PhD dissertation, Stanford University.

Rieff, David. 1990. Review of *Migrant Souls. Los Angeles Times,* January 28, 3.

Román, David. 1993. "Arturo Islas (1938–1991)." In *Contemporary Gay American Novelists: A Bio-Bibliographical Critical Sourcebook,* edited by Emmanuel S. Nelson, 220–25. Westport: Greenwood.

Rosaldo, Renato. 1991. "Fables of the Fallen Guy." In *Criticism in the Borderland: Studies in Chicano Literature, Culture, and Ideology,* edited by Héctor Calderón and José David Saldívar, 84–93. Durham: Duke University Press.

Ruiz, Vicki. 1984. Review of *The Rain God. El Paso Herald-Post,* October 12, 1984.

Sáenz, Benjamin. 1990. "Incarnations of the Border." *Ambiente,* 13.

Saldívar, José David. 1991. *The Dialectics of Our Americas: Genealogy, Cultural Critique and Literary History.* Durham: Duke University Press.

———. 1997. *Border Matters.* Berkeley and Los Angeles: University of California Press.

Sánchez, Marta. E. 1990. "Arturo Islas's *The Rain God:* An Alternative Tradition." *American Literature* 62, no. 2:284–304.

Sánchez, Rosaura. 1991. "Ideological Discourses in Islas's *The Rain God.*" In *Criticism in the Borderland: Studies in Chicano Literature, Culture, and Ideology,* edited by Héctor Calderón and José David Saldívar, 114–26. Durham: Duke University Press.

Sedgwick, Eve K. 1990. *Epistemology of the Closet.* Berkeley and Los Angeles: University of California Press.

Shorris, Earl. 1992. *Latinos: A Biography of the People.* New York: W. W Norton.

Unger, David. 1990. Review of *Migrant Souls. New York Times,* May 20, 30.

Velásquez-Treviño, Gloria. 1992. "Arturo." *Bilingual Review* 17, no. 2:168.

Villescas, José Jr. 2000. Opinion. *El Paso Times,* October 14, 13A.

Womack, John. 1972. "The Chicano." *New York Review of Books,* August 31, 12–18.

Index

self, sense of, 22–23, 33, 99, 108, 112, 124
self-as-narrator, 18, 109
self-destructive behavior: alcohol abuse as, 116, 119; family and, 23, 71; gay sexuality and, 80, 83, 94; writing and, 60, 71, 94. *See also* self-mutilation
self-determination, 12–13
self-hatred, 37, 68, 80–81, 88
selfless love, 83
self-mutilation, 37, 38, 110
Sequoia, 35
Seventh Day Adventists, 10–11, 103
sexual abuse, 10, 126
Shakespeare, William, 131
shared dreaming, 89
Shorris, Earl, 7, 14–15, 132, 167–68n1
short stories, 33–38, 109
"six," 45–46
Skenazy, Paul, 44, 54–55
Smith Corona typewriter, 49
sociosexual transformations, 82, 84–86, 171n1
Sontag, Susan, 61
Soul on Ice (Cleaver), 137
Southern gothic narrative realism, 48
South of Market (San Francisco), 85, 121
Sowell, Thomas, 144
Spanish/*indio* duality, 3–4, 8–9, 37–38, 63, 129
Spears, Jay, 90–96; alcohol abuse and, 116–17, 119; death of, 100–101, 121, 171n2; "The Lame" and, 53; Louie and, 21; Mario and, 22–23; physical disability and, 91, 96, 115; in poetry, 68–70; reconciliation with, 100–101, 160; therapy and, 73, 97–99; tyrant/victim relationship and, 15, 23, 89, 90, 92, 93–96
Spicer, Jack, 171n1
spirit/body duality, 14
Stand and Deliver, 144
Stanford Directions (periodical), 86
Stanford Medical Health Center, 111–12, 123, 172n1
Stanford Sexual Rights Forum, 82, 135
Stanford University: Chicano/a studies at, 26–30, 172n1; culture wars at, 142–46; graduate student at, 20, 30–31, 81–85, 108–9, 114, 135–37; HIV-AIDS and, 123, 127; physical disability and, 108–10, 114–15, 117–18, 172n1; professor at, 23, 137–57, 170n11, 172–73nn3–5; tenure at, 32–33, 38–39, 43, 139, 142–43; undergraduate at, 1, 35, 75, 78–80, 107, 133–35
STDs, 111, 123
Stegner, Wallace, 30, 43, 46, 114
Stendhal, 48

stereotypes, 42, 49, 84, 171n1
St. Luke's Hospital, 100
Stonewall riots, 85
storytelling traditions, 46, 47–48
St. Patrick's Cathedral (El Paso, Tex.), 9–10
Strauss, Roger, 39
student council president, 12
student protests, 139–40
substance abuse. *See* alcohol abuse; drug abuse
suicidal tendencies, 23, 68, 80, 92, 97–98, 117
Suppes, Patrick, 43
Supreme Court, 171n1
surveillance, 34, 36, 102, 115
symbolism, 36, 64
syphilis, 123
Syrians, 131–32

Tan, Amy, 60
Tatum, Charles, 27
teaching, 32–33, 146–57, 170n11, 172–73nn3–5
team-teaching, 27–28
tenure, 32–33, 38–39, 43, 139, 142–43
therapy sessions, 17–19, 23, 97–99
third-person narratives, 35, 36, 40–41, 57
This Side of Paradise (Fitzgerald), 58, 149, 150
Thomas, Piri, 40
time perception, 125–26
Tláloc, 46
Tlatelolco Massacre, 136
Tolstoy, Leo, 148
Tonatiuh International, 172n2
top/bottom erotic play, 96, 113, 115
"The Totality of Male Domination vs. Sexual Pleasure" (Cazares), 28
transvestism, 65, 70–71
Tropic of Cancer (Miller), 171n1
tuberculosis, 5, 170n11
Turgenev, 48
Twain, Mark, 152, 153
typewriters, 49
tyrant/victim relationships: Bergh and, 83, 94; in "Día de los muertos," 92; parents and, 14–15, 17–18, 23, 93; S&M scene and, 89–90; Spears and, 15, 23, 89, 90, 92, 93–96

ulcerative colitis, 90, 103, 111–12, 170n11. *See also* colostomy
undocumented workers, 34
United Farm Workers, 136
University of California-Berkeley, 137
University of California-Santa Cruz, 44, 54
University of New Mexico Press, 56

Indexer:	Sharon Sweeney
Text:	10/14 Palatino
Display:	Univers Condensed Light 47 and Bauer Bodoni
Compositor, Printer, and Binder:	Sheridan Books, Inc.